ISBN: 9781313027281

Published by:
HardPress Publishing
8345 NW 66TH ST #2561
MIAMI FL 33166-2626

Email: info@hardpress.net
Web: http://www.hardpress.net

AUNT JANE OF KENTUCKY

Aunt Jane
of Kentucky

BY

ELIZA CALVERT HALL

With a Frontispiece and Page Decorations by
BEULAH STRONG

Boston
Little, Brown, and Company
1907

𝔓rinters
S. J. PARKHILL & CO., BOSTON, U. S. A.

TO

MY MOTHER AND FATHER

I Dedicate this Book

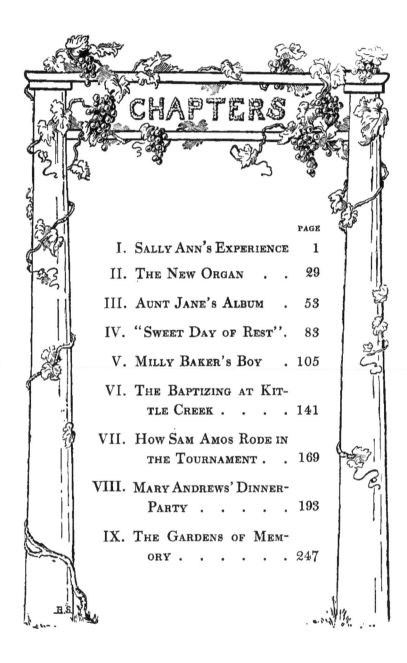

CHAPTERS

"THERE is not an existence about us but at first seems colorless, dreary, lethargic: what can our soul have in common with that of an elderly spinster, a slow-witted plowman, a miser who worships his gold? . . . . But . . . . the emotion that lived and died in an old-fashioned country parlor shall as mightily stir our heart, shall as unerringly find its way to the deepest sources of life as the majestic passion that ruled the life of a king and shed its triumphant luster from the dazzling height of a throne." — *Maeterlinck.*

I

SALLY ANN'S EXPERIENCE

I

SALLY ANN'S EXPERIENCE

"COME right in and set down. I was jest wishin' I had somebody to talk to. Take that chair right by the door so's you can get the breeze."

And Aunt Jane beamed at me over her silver-rimmed spectacles and hitched her own chair a little to one side, in order to give me the full benefit of the wind that was blowing softly through the white-curtained window, and carrying into the room the heavenliest odors from a field of clover that lay in full bloom just across the road. For it was June in Kentucky, and clover and blue-grass were running sweet riot over the face of the earth.

Aunt Jane and her room together always carried me back to a dead and gone generation. There was a rag carpet on the floor, of the "hit-or-miss" pattern; the chairs were ancient Shaker rockers, some with homely "shuck" bottoms, and each had a tidy of snowy thread or crochet cotton fastened primly over the back. The high bed and bureau and a shining mahogany table suggested an era of "plain living" far, far remote from the day of Turkish rugs and Japanese bric-a-brac, and Aunt Jane was in perfect correspondence with her environment. She wore a purple calico dress, rather short and scant; a gingham apron, with a capacious pocket, in which she always carried knitting or some other "handy work"; a white handkerchief was laid primly around the wrinkled throat and fastened with a pin containing a lock of gray hair; her cap was of black lace and lutestring ribbon, not one of the butterfly affairs that perch on the top of the puffs and frizzes of the modern old lady, but a

4

substantial structure that covered her whole head and was tied securely under her chin. She talked in a sweet old treble with a little lisp, caused by the absence of teeth, and her laugh was as clear and joyous as a young girl's.

"Yes, I'm a-piecin' quilts again," she said, snipping away at the bits of calico in her lap. "I did say I was done with that sort o' work; but this mornin' I was rummagin' around up in the garret, and I come across this bundle of pieces, and thinks I, 'I reckon it's intended for me to piece one more quilt before I die;' I must 'a' put 'em there thirty years ago and clean forgot 'em, and I've been settin' here all the evenin' cuttin' 'em and thinkin' about old times.

"Jest feel o' that," she continued, tossing some scraps into my lap. "There ain't any such caliker nowadays. This ain't your five-cent stuff that fades in the first washin' and wears out in the second. A caliker dress was somethin' worth buyin' and worth makin' up in them days. That blue-flowered piece was a dress I got the spring before Abram died. When I put on mournin' it was as good as new, and I give it to sister Mary. That one with the green ground and white figger was my niece Rebecca's. She wore it for the first time to

5

the County Fair the year I took the premium on my salt-risin' bread and sponge cake. This black-an'-white piece Sally Ann Flint give me. I ricollect 'twas in blackberry time, and I'd been out in the big pasture pickin' some for supper, and I stopped in at Sally Ann's for a drink o' water on my way back. She was cuttin' out this dress."

Aunt Jane broke off with a little soprano laugh.

"Did I ever tell you about Sally Ann's experience?" she said, as she laid two three-cornered pieces together and began to sew with her slender, nervous old fingers.

To find Aunt Jane alone and in a reminiscent mood! This was delightful.

"Do tell me," I said.

Aunt Jane was silent for a few moments. She always made this pause before beginning a story, and there was something impressive about it. I used to think she was making an invocation to the goddess of Memory.

"'Twas forty years ago," she began musingly, "and the way of it was this. Our church was considerably out o' fix. It needed a new roof. Some o' the winder lights was out, and the floor was as bare as your hand, and always had been. The men folks managed to git

6

the roof shingled and the winders fixed, and us women in the Mite Society concluded we'd git a cyarpet. We'd been savin' up our money for some time, and we had about twelve dollars. I ricollect what a argument we had, for some of us wanted the cyarpet, and some wanted to give it to furrin missions, as we'd set out to do at first. Sally Ann was the one that settled it. She says at last — Sally Ann was in favor of the cyarpet — she says, 'Well, if any of the heathen fails to hear the gospel on account of our gittin' this cyarpet, they'll be saved anyhow, so Parson Page says. And if we send the money and they do hear the gospel, like as not they won't repent, and then they're certain to be damned. And it seems to me as long as we ain't sure what they'll do, we might as well keep the money and git the cyarpet. I never did see much sense anyhow,' says she, 'in givin' people a chance to damn theirselves.'

"Well, we decided to take Sally Ann's advice, and we was talkin' about app'intin' a committee to go to town the follerin' Monday and pick out the cyarpet, when all at once 'Lizabeth Taylor — she was our treasurer — she spoke up, and says she, 'There ain't any use app'intin' that committee. The money's gone,' she says, sort o' short and quick. 'I kept it in my top bureau drawer, and when I went for it yesterday, it was gone. I'll pay it back if I'm ever able, but I ain't able now.' And with that she got up and walked out o' the room, before any one could say a word, and we seen her goin' down the road lookin' straight before her and walkin' right fast.

"And we — we set there and stared at each other in a sort o' dazed way. I could see that everybody was thinkin' the same thing, but nobody said a word, till our minister's wife — she was as good a woman as ever lived — she says, '*Judge not.*'

"Them two words was jest like a sermon to us. Then Sally Ann spoke up and says: 'For the Lord's sake, don't let the men folks know anything about this. They're always sayin' that women ain't fit to handle money, and I for one don't want to give 'em any more ground to stand on than they've already got.'

"So we agreed to say nothin' about it, and all of us kept our promise except Milly Amos. She had mighty little sense to begin with, and havin' been married only about two months, she'd about lost that little. So next mornin' I happened to meet Sam Amos, and he says to me, 'Aunt Jane, how much money have you women got to'rds the new cyarpet for the church?' I looked him

square in the face, and I says, 'Are you a member of the
Ladies' Mite Society of Goshen church, Sam Amos?
For if you are, you already know how much money we've
got, and if you ain't, you've got no business knowin'.
And, furthermore,' says I, 'there's some women that
can't keep a secret and a promise, and some that can,
and *I* can.' And that settled *him*.

"Well, 'Lizabeth never showed her face outside her
door for more'n a month afterwards, and a more pitiful-
lookin' creatur' you never saw than she was when she
come out to prayer-meetin' the night Sally Ann give her
experience. She set 'way back in the church, and she
was as pale and peaked as if she had been through a
siege of typhoid. I ricollect it all as if it had been yesterday. We sung 'Sweet Hour of Prayer,' and Parson Page
prayed, and then called on the brethren to say anything
they might feel called on to say concernin' their experience in the past week. Old Uncle Jim Matthews begun
to clear his throat, and I knew, as well as I knew my
name, he was fixin' to git up and tell how precious the
Lord had been to his soul, jest like he'd been doin' every
Wednesday night for twenty years. But before he got
started, here come 'Lizabeth walkin' down the side aisle
and stopped right in front o' the pulpit.

9

"'I've somethin' to say,' she says. 'It's been on my mind till I can't stand it any longer. I've got to tell it, or I'll go crazy. It was me that took that cyarpet money. I only meant to borrow it. I thought sure I'd be able to pay it back before it was wanted. But things went wrong, and I ain't known a peaceful minute since, and never shall again, I reckon. I took it to pay my way up to Louisville, the time I got the news that Mary was dyin'.'

"Mary was her daughter by her first husband, you see. 'I begged Jacob to give me the money to go on,' says she, 'and he wouldn't do it. I tried to give up and stay, but I jest couldn't. Mary was all I had in the world; and maybe you that has children can put yourself in my place, and know what it would be to hear your only child callin' to you from her death-bed, and you not able to go to her. I asked Jacob three times for the money,' she says, 'and when I found he wouldn't give it to me, I said to myself, "I'm goin' anyhow." I got down on my knees,' says she, 'and asked the Lord to show me a way, and I felt sure he would. As soon as Jacob had eat his breakfast and gone out on the farm, I dressed myself, and as I opened the top bureau drawer to get out my best collar, I saw the missionary

10

money. It come right into my head,' says she, 'that maybe this was the answer to my prayer; maybe I could borrow this money, and pay it back some way or other before it was called for.   I tried to put it out o' my head, but the thought kept comin' back; and when I went down into the sittin'-room to get Jacob's cyarpetbag to carry a few things in, I happened to look up at the mantelpiece and saw the brass candlesticks with prisms all 'round 'em that used to belong to my mother; and all at once I seemed to see jest what the Lord intended for me to do.

"'You know,' she says, 'I had a boarder summer before last — that lady from Louisville — and she wanted them candlesticks the worst kind, and offered me fifteen dollars for 'em. I wouldn't part with 'em then, but she said if ever I wanted to sell 'em, to let her know, and she left her name and address on a cyard. I went to the big Bible and got out the cyard, and I packed the candlesticks in the cyarpetbag, and put on my bonnet. When I opened the door I looked up the road, and the first thing I saw was Dave Crawford comin' along in his new buggy. I went out to the gate, and he drew up and asked me if I was goin' to town, and said he'd take me. It looked like the Lord was leadin' me all the time,' says she, 'but the way things turned out it must 'a' been Satan. I got to Mary just two hours before she died, and she looked up in my face and says, "Mother, I knew God wouldn't let me die till I'd seen you once more." ' "

Here Aunt Jane took off her glasses and wiped her eyes.

"'I can't tell this without cryin' to save my life," said she; "but 'Lizabeth never shed a tear. She looked like she'd got past cryin', and she talked straight on as if she'd made up her mind to say jest so much, and she'd die if she didn't git to say it.

"''As soon as the funeral was over,' says she, 'I set out to find the lady that wanted the candlesticks. She wasn't at home, but her niece was there, and said she'd heard her aunt speak of the candlesticks often; and she'd be home in a few days and would send me the money right off. I come home thinkin' it was all right, and I kept expectin' the money every day, but it never come till day before yesterday. I wrote three times about it, but I never got a word from her till Monday. She had just got home, she said, and hoped I hadn't been inconvenienced by the delay. She wrote a nice, polite letter and sent me a check for fifteen dollars, and here it is. I wanted to confess it all that day at the Mite Society, but somehow I couldn't till I had the money right in my hand to pay back. If the lady had only come back when her niece said she was comin', it would all have turned out right, but I reckon it's a judgment on me for meddling with the Lord's money. God only knows what I've suffered,' says she, 'but if I had to do it over again, I believe I'd do it. Mary was all the child I had in the world, and I had to see her once more before she died. I've been a member of this church for twenty years,' says she, 'but I reckon you'll have to turn me out now.'

"The pore thing stood there tremblin' and holdin' out the check as if she expected somebody to come and take it. Old Silas Petty was glowerin' at her from under his eyebrows, and it put me in mind of the Pharisees and the woman they wanted to stone, and I ricollect thinkin', 'Oh, if the Lord Jesus would jest come in and take her part!' And while we all set there like a passel o' mutes, Sally Ann got up and marched down the middle aisle and stood right by 'Lizabeth. You know what funny thoughts people will have sometimes.

"Well, I felt so relieved. It popped into my head all at once that we didn't need the Lord after all, Sally

13

Ann would do jest as well. It seemed sort o' like sacrilege, but I couldn't help it.

"Well, Sally Ann looked all around as composed as you please, and says she, 'I reckon if anybody's turned out o' this church on account o' that miserable little money, it'll be Jacob and not 'Lizabeth. A man that won't give his wife money to go to her dyin' child is too mean to stay in a Christian church anyhow; and I'd like to know how it is that a woman, that had eight hundred dollars when she married, has to go to her husband and git down on her knees and beg for what's her own. Where's that money 'Lizabeth had when she married you?' says she, turnin' round and lookin' Jacob in the face. 'Down in that ten-acre medder lot, ain't it? — and in that new barn you built last spring. A pretty elder you are, ain't you? Elders don't seem to have improved much since Susannah's times. If there ain't one sort o' meanness in 'em it's another,' says she.

"Goodness knows what she would 'a' said, but jest here old Deacon Petty rose up. And says he, 'Brethren,' — and he spread his arms out and waved 'em up and down like he was goin' to pray, — 'brethren, this is awful! If this woman wants to give her religious experience,

14

why,' says he, very kind and condescendin', 'of course she can do so. But when it comes to *a woman* standin' up in the house of the Lord and revilin' an elder as this woman is doin', why, I tremble,' says he, 'for the church of Christ. For don't the Apostle Paul say, "Let your women keep silence in the church"?'

"As soon as he named the 'Postle Paul, Sally Ann give a kind of snort. Sally Ann was terrible free-spoken. And when Deacon Petty said that, she jest squared herself like she intended to stand there till judgment day, and says she, 'The 'Postle Paul has been dead ruther too long for me to be afraid of him. And I never heard of him app'intin' Deacon Petty to represent him in this church. If the 'Postle Paul don't like what I'm sayin', let him rise up from his grave in Corinthians or Ephesians, or wherever he's buried, and say so. I've got a message from the Lord to the men folks of this church, and I'm goin' to deliver it, Paul or no Paul,' says she. 'And as for you, Silas Petty, I ain't forgot the time I dropped in to see Maria one Saturday night and found her washin' out her flannel petticoat and dryin' it before the fire. And every time I've had to hear you lead in prayer since then I've said to myself, "Lord, how high can a man's prayers rise toward heaven when his wife ain't got but one flannel skirt to her name? No higher than the back of his pew, if you'll let me tell it." I knew jest how it was,' said Sally Ann, 'as well as if Maria'd told me. She'd been havin' the milk and butter money from the old roan cow she'd raised from a little heifer, and jest because feed was scarce, you'd sold her off before Maria had money enough to buy her winter flannels. I can give my experience, can I? Well, that's jest what I'm a-doin',' says she; 'and while I'm about it,' says she, 'I'll give in some experience for 'Lizabeth and Maria and the rest of the women who, betwixt their husbands an' the 'Postle Paul, have about lost all the gumption and grit that the Lord started them out with. If the 'Postle Paul,' says she, 'has got anything to say about a woman workin' like a slave for twenty-five years and then havin' to set up an' wash out her clothes Saturday night, so's she can go to church clean Sunday mornin', I'd like to hear it. But don't you dare to say anything to me about keepin' silence in the church. There was times when Paul says he didn't know whether he had the Spirit of God or not, and I'm certain that when he wrote that text he wasn't any more inspired than you are, Silas Petty, when you tell Maria to shut her mouth.'

16

SALLY ANN'S EXPERIENCE

"Job Taylor was settin' right in front of Deacon Petty, and I reckon he thought his time was comin' next; so he gets up, easy-like, with his red bandanna to his mouth, and starts out. But Sally Ann headed him off before he'd gone six steps, and says she, 'There ain't anything the matter with you, Job Taylor; you set right down and hear what I've got to say. I've knelt and stood through enough o' your long-winded prayers, and now it's my time to talk and yours to listen.'

"And bless your life, if Job didn't set down as meek as Moses, and Sally Ann lit right into him. And says she, 'I reckon you're afraid I'll tell some o' your meanness, ain't you? And the only thing that stands in my way is that there's so much to tell I don't know where to begin. There ain't a woman in this church,' says she, 'that don't know how Marthy scrimped and worked and saved to buy her a new set o' furniture, and how you took the money with you when you went to Cincinnata, the spring before she died, and come back without the furniture. And when she asked you for the money, you told her that she and everything she had belonged to you, and that your mother's old furniture was good enough for anybody. It's my belief,' says she, 'that's what killed Marthy. Women are

17

dyin' every day, and the doctors will tell you it's some new-fangled disease or other, when, if the truth was known, it's nothin' but wantin' somethin' they can't git, and hopin' and waitin' for somethin' that never comes. I've watched 'em, and I know. The night before Marthy died she says to me, "Sally Ann," says she, "I could die a heap peacefuler if I jest knew the front room was fixed up right with a new set of furniture for the funeral."' And Sally Ann p'inted her finger right at Job and says she, 'I said it then, and I say it now to your face, Job Taylor, you killed Marthy the same as if you'd taken her by the throat and choked the life out of her.'

"Mary Embry, Job's sister-in-law, was settin' right behind me, and I heard her say, 'Amen!' as fervent as if somebody had been prayin'. Job set there, lookin' like a sheep-killin' dog, and Sally Ann went right on. 'I know,' says she, 'the law gives you the right to your wives' earnin's and everything they've got, down to the clothes on their backs; and I've always said there was some Kentucky law that was made for the express purpose of encouragin' men in their natural meanness, — a p'int in which the Lord knows they don't need no encouragin'. There's some men,' says she, 'that'll sneak behind the 'Postle Paul when they're plannin' any meanness against their wives, and some that runs to the law, and you're one of the law kind. But mark my words,' says she, 'one of these days, you men who've been stealin' your wives' property and defraudin' 'em, and cheatin' 'em out o' their just dues, you'll have to stand before a Judge that cares mighty little for Kentucky law; and all the law and all the Scripture you can bring up won't save you from goin' where the rich man went.'

"I can see Sally Ann right now," and Aunt Jane pushed her glasses up on her forehead, and looked with a dreamy, retrospective gaze through the doorway and beyond, where swaying elms and maples were whispering softly to each other as the breeze touched them. "She had on her old black poke-bonnet and some black yarn mitts, and she didn't come nigh up to Job's shoulder, but Job set and listened as if he jest *had to*. I heard Dave Crawford shufflin' his feet and clearin' his throat while Sally Ann was talkin' to Job. Dave's farm j'ined Sally Ann's, and they had a lawsuit once about the way a fence ought to run, and Sally Ann beat him. He always despised Sally Ann after that, and used to call her a 'he-woman.' Sally Ann heard

19

the shufflin', and as soon as she got through with Job, she turned around to Dave, and says she: 'Do you think your hemmin' and scrapin' is goin' to stop me, Dave Crawford? You're one o' the men that makes me think that it's better to be a Kentucky horse than a Kentucky woman. Many's the time,' says she, 'I've seen pore July with her head tied up, crawlin' around tryin' to cook for sixteen harvest hands, and you out in the stable cossetin' up a sick mare, and rubbin' down your three-year-olds to get 'em in trim for the fair. Of all the things that's hard to understand,' says she, 'the hardest is a man that has more mercy on his horse than he has on his wife. July's found rest at last,' says she, 'out in the graveyard; and every time I pass your house I thank the Lord that you've got to pay a good price for your cookin' now, as there ain't a woman in the country fool enough to step into July's shoes.'

"But, la!" said Aunt Jane, breaking off with her happy laugh, — the laugh of one who revels in rich memories, — "what's the use of me tellin' all this stuff? The long and the short of it is, that Sally Ann had her say about nearly every man in the church. She told how Mary Embry had to cut up her weddin'

skirts to make clothes for her first baby; and how John
Martin stopped Hannah one day when she was carryin' her mother a pound of butter, and made her go
back and put the butter down in the cellar; and how
Lije Davison used to make Ann pay him for every
bit of chicken feed, and then take half the egg
money because the chickens got into his garden;
and how Abner Page give his wife twenty-five cents
for spendin' money the time she went to visit her
sister.

"Sally Ann always was a masterful sort of woman,
and that night it seemed like she was possessed. The
way she talked made me think of the Day of Pente-
cost and the gift of tongues. And finally she got to
the minister! I'd been wonderin' all along if she was
goin' to let him off. She turned around to where he
was settin' under the pulpit, and says she, 'Brother
Page, you're a good man, but you ain't so good you
couldn't be better. It was jest last week,' says she,
'that the women come around beggin' money to buy
you a new suit of clothes to go to Presbytery in; and
I told 'em if it was to get Mis' Page a new dress, I was
ready to give; but not a dime was I goin' to give towards puttin' finery on a man's back. I'm tired o'

seein' the ministers walk up into the pulpit in their slick black broadcloths, and their wives settin' down in the pew in an old black silk that's been turned upside down, wrong side out, and hind part before, and sponged, and pressed, and made over till you can't tell whether it's silk, or caliker, or what.'

"Well, I reckon there was some o' the women that expected the roof to fall down on us when Sally Ann said that right to the minister. But it didn't fall, and Sally Ann went straight on. 'And when it comes to the perseverance of the saints and the decrees of God,' says she, 'there ain't many can preach a better sermon; but there's some of your sermons,' says she, 'that ain't fit for much but kindlin' fires. There's that one you preached last Sunday on the twenty-fourth verse of the fifth chapter of Ephesians. I reckon I've heard about a hundred and fifty sermons on that text, and I reckon I'll keep on hearin' 'em as long as there ain't anybody but men to do the preachin'. Anybody would think,' says she, 'that you preachers was struck blind every time you git through with the twenty-fourth verse, for I never heard a sermon on the twenty-fifth verse. I believe there's men in this church that thinks the fifth chapter of Ephesians hasn't got but twenty-four verses, and I'm goin' to read the rest of it to 'em for once anyhow.'

"And if Sally Ann didn't walk right up into the pulpit same as if she'd been ordained, and read what Paul said about men lovin' their wives as Christ loved the church, and as they loved their own bodies.

" 'Now,' says she, 'if Brother Page can reconcile these texts with what Paul says about women submittin' and bein' subject, he's welcome to do it. But,' says she, 'if I had the preachin' to do, I wouldn't waste time reconcilin'. I'd jest say that when Paul told women to be subject to their husbands in everything, he wasn't inspired; and when he told men to love their wives as their own bodies, he was inspired; and I'd like to see the Presbytery that could silence me from preachin' as long as I wanted to preach. As for turnin' out o' the church,' says she, 'I'd like to know who's to do the turnin' out. When the disciples brought that woman to Christ there wasn't a man in the crowd fit to cast a stone at her; and if there's any man nowadays good enough to set in judgment on a woman, his name ain't on the rolls of Goshen church. If 'Lizabeth,' says she, 'had as much common sense as she's got conscience, she'd know that the matter o' that

23

money didn't concern nobody but our Mite Society, and we women can settle it without any help from you deacons and elders.'

"Well, I reckon Parson Page thought if he didn't head Sally Ann off some way or other she'd go on all night; so when she kind o' stopped for breath and shut up the big Bible, he grabbed a hymn-book and says:

"'Let us sing "Blest be the Tie that Binds."'

"He struck up the tune himself; and about the middle of the first verse Mis' Page got up and went over to where 'Lizabeth was standin', and give her the right hand of fellowship, and then Mis' Petty did the same; and first thing we knew we was all around her shakin' hands and huggin' her and cryin' over her. 'Twas a reg'lar love-feast; and we went home feelin' like we'd been through a big protracted meetin' and got religion over again.

"'Twasn't more'n a week till 'Lizabeth was down with slow fever — nervous collapse, old Dr. Pendleton called it. We took turns nursin' her, and one day she looked up in my face and says, 'Jane, I know now what the mercy of the Lord is.'"

Here Aunt Jane paused, and began to cut three-cornered pieces out of a time-stained square of flowered chintz. The quilt was to be of the wild-goose pattern. There was a drowsy hum from the bee-hive near the window, and the shadows were lengthening as sunset approached.

"One queer thing about it," she resumed, "was that while Sally Ann was talkin', not one of us felt like laughin'. We set there as solemn as if parson was preachin' to us on 'lection and predestination. But whenever I think about it now, I laugh fit to kill. And I've thought many a time that Sally Ann's plain talk to them men done more good than all the sermons us women had had preached to us about bein' 'shame-faced' and 'submittin'' ourselves to our husbands, for every one o' them women come out in new clothes that spring, and such a change as it made in some of 'em! I wouldn't be surprised if she did have a message to deliver, jest as she said. The Bible says an ass spoke up once and reproved a man, and I reckon if an ass can reprove a man, so can a woman. And it looks to me like men stand in need of reprovin' now as much as they did in Balaam's days.

"Jacob died the follerin' fall, and 'Lizabeth got shed of her troubles. The triflin' scamp never married her for anything but her money.

"Things is different from what they used to be," she went on, as she folded her pieces into a compact bundle and tied it with a piece of gray yarn. "My son-in-law was tellin' me last summer how a passel o' women kept goin' up to Frankfort and so pesterin' the Legislatur', that they had to change the laws to git rid of 'em. So married women now has all the property rights they want, and more'n some of 'em has sense to use, I reckon."

"How about you and Uncle Abram?" I suggested. "Didn't Sally Ann say anything about you in her experience?"

Aunt Jane's black eyes snapped with some of the fire of her long-past youth. "La! no, child," she said. "Abram never was that kind of a man, and I never was that kind of a woman. I ricollect as we was walkin' home that night Abram says, sort o' humble-like: 'Jane, hadn't you better git that brown merino you was lookin' at last County Court day?'

"And I says, 'Don't you worry about that brown merino, Abram. It's a-lyin' in my bottom drawer right now. I told the storekeeper to cut it off jest as soon as your back was turned, and Mis' Simpson is goin' to make it next week.' And Abram he jest

laughed, and says, 'Well, Jane, I never saw your beat.'
You see, I never was any hand at 'submittin'' myself
to my husband, like some women. I've often wondered if Abram wouldn't 'a' been jest like Silas Petty
if I'd been like Maria. I've noticed that whenever a
woman's willin' to be imposed upon, there's always
a man standin' 'round ready to do the imposin'. I
never went to a law-book to find out what my rights
was. I did my duty faithful to Abram, and when I
wanted anything I went and got it, and Abram paid
for it, and I can't see but what we got on jest as well
as we'd 'a' done if I'd a-'submitted' myself."

Longer and longer grew the shadows, and the faint
tinkle of bells came in through the windows. The
cows were beginning to come home. The spell of
Aunt Jane's dramatic art was upon me. I began to
feel that my own personality had somehow slipped
away from me, and those dead people, evoked from
their graves by an old woman's histrionism, seemed
more real to me than my living, breathing self.

"There now, I've talked you clean to death," she
said with a happy laugh, as I rose to go. "But we've
had a real nice time, and I'm glad you come."

The sun was almost down as I walked slowly away.

When I looked back, at the turn of the road, Aunt Jane was standing on the doorstep, shading her eyes and peering across the level fields. I knew what it meant. Beyond the fields was a bit of woodland, and in one corner of that you might, if your eyesight was good, discern here and there a glimpse of white. It was the old burying-ground of Goshen church; and I knew by the strained attitude and intent gaze of the watcher in the door that somewhere in the sunlit space between Aunt Jane's doorstep and the little country graveyard, the souls of the living and the dead were keeping a silent tryst.

II

THE NEW ORGAN

II

THE NEW ORGAN

"GITTIN' a new organ is a mighty different thing nowadays from what it was when I was young," said Aunt Jane judicially, as she lifted a panful of yellow harvest apples from the table and began to peel them for dumplings.

Potatoes, peas, and asparagus were bubbling on the stove, and the dumplings were in honor of the invited guest, who had begged the privilege of staying in the kitchen awhile. Aunt Jane was one of those rare housekeepers whose kitchens are more attractive than the parlors of other people.

"And gittin' religion is different, too," she continued, propping her feet on the round of a chair for the greater comfort and convenience of her old knees. "Both of 'em is a heap easier than they used to be, and the organs is a heap better. I don't know whether the religion's any better or not. You know I went up to my daughter Mary Frances' last week; and the folks up there was havin' a big meetin' in the Tabernicle, and that's how come me to be thinkin' about organs.

"The preacher was an evangelist, as they call him, Sam Joynes, from 'way down South. In my day he'd 'a' been called the Rev. Samuel Joynes. Folks didn't call their preachers Tom, Dick, and Harry, and Jim and Sam, like they do now. I'd like to 'a' seen anybody callin' Parson Page 'Lem Page.' He was the Rev. Lemuel Page, and don't you forget it. But things is different, as I said awhile ago, and even the little boys says 'Sam Joynes,' jest like he played marbles with 'em every day. I went to the Tabernicle three or four times; and of all the preachers that ever I heard, he certainly is the beatenest. Why, I ain't laughed so much since me and Abram went to Barnum's circus, the year before the war. He was preachin' one day about cleanliness bein' next to godliness, which it certainly is, and he says, 'You old skunk, you!' But, la! the worse names he called 'em the better they 'peared to like it, and sinners was converted wholesale every time he preached. But there wasn't no goin' to the mourners' bench and mournin' for your sins and havin' people prayin' and cryin' over you. They jest set and laughed and grinned while he was gittin' off his jokes, and then they'd go up and shake hands with him, and there they was all saved and ready to be baptized and taken into the church."

Just here the old yellow rooster fluttered up to the door-step and gave a hoarse, ominous crow.

"There, now! You hear that?" said Aunt Jane, as she tossed him a golden peeling from her pan. "There's some folks that gives right up and looks for sickness or death or bad news every time a rooster crows in the door. But I never let such things bother me. The Bible says that nobody knows what a day may bring forth, and if I don't know, it ain't likely my old yeller rooster does.

"What was I talkin' about? Oh, yes — the big meetin'. Well, I never was any hand to say that old ways is best, and I don't say so now. If you can convert a man by callin' him a polecat, why, call him one, of course. And mournin' ain't always a sign o' true repentance. They used to tell how Silas Petty mourned for forty days, and, as Sally Ann said, he had about as much religion as old Dan Tucker's Derby ram.

"However, it was the organ I set out to tell about. It's jest like me to wander away from the p'int. Abram always said a text would have to be made like a postage stamp for me to stick to it. You see, they'd jest got a fine new organ at Mary Frances' church, and she was tellin' me how they paid for it. One man give five hundred dollars, and another give three hundred; then they collected four or five hundred amongst the other members, and give a lawn party and a strawberry festival and raised another hundred. It set me to thinkin' o' the time us women got the organ for Goshen church. It wasn't any light matter, for, besides the money it took us nearly three years to raise, there was the opposition. Come to think of it, we raised more opposition than we did money."

And Aunt Jane laughed a blithe laugh and tossed

another peeling to the yellow rooster, who had dropped the rôle of harbinger of evil and was posing as a humble suppliant.

"An organ in them days, honey, was jest a wedge to split the church half in two. It was the new cyarpet that brought on the organ. You know how it is with yourself; you git a new dress, and then you've got to have a new bonnet, and then you can't wear your old shoes and gloves with a new dress and a new bonnet, and the first thing you know you've spent five times as much as you set out to spend. That's the way it was with us about the cyarpet and the organ and the pulpit chairs and the communion set.

"Most o' the men folks was against the organ from the start, and Silas Petty was the foremost. Silas made a p'int of goin' against everything that women favored. Sally Ann used to say that if a woman was to come up to him and say, 'Le's go to heaven,' Silas would start off towards the other place right at once; he was jest that mulish and contrairy. He met Sally Ann one day, and says he, 'Jest give you women rope enough and you'll turn the house o' the Lord into a reg'lar toy-shop.' And Sally Ann she says, 'You'd better go home, Silas, and read the book of Exodus. If the

Lord told Moses how to build the Tabernicle with the goats' skins and rams' skins and blue and purple and scarlet and fine linen and candlesticks with six branches, I reckon he won't object to a few yards o' cyarpetin' and a little organ in Goshen church.'

"Sally Ann always had an answer ready, and I used to think she knew more about the Bible than Parson Page did himself.

"Of course Uncle Jim Matthews didn't want the organ; he was afraid it might interfere with his singin'. Job Taylor always stood up for Silas, so he didn't want it; and Parson Page never opened his mouth one way or the other. He was one o' those men that tries to set on both sides o' the fence at once, and he'd set that way so long he was a mighty good hand at balancin' himself.

"Us women didn't say much, but we made up our minds to have the organ. So we went to work in the Mite Society, and in less'n three years we had enough money to git it. I've often wondered how many pounds o' butter and how many baskets of eggs it took to raise that money. I reckon if they'd 'a' been piled up on top of each other they'd 'a' reached to the top o' the steeple. The women of Israel brought

their ear-rings and bracelets to help build the Tabernicle, but we had jest our egg and butter money, and
the second year, when the chicken cholery was so
bad, our prospects looked mighty blue.

"When I saw that big organ up at Danville, I couldn't
help thinkin' about the little thing we worked so hard
to git. 'Twasn't much bigger'n a washstand, and I
reckon if I was to hear it now, I'd think it was mighty
feeble and squeaky. But it sounded fine enough to us
in them days, and, little as it was, it raised a disturbance
for miles around.

"When it come down from Louisville, Abram went
to town with his two-horse wagon and brought it out
and set it up in our parlor. My Jane had been takin'
lessons in town all winter, so's to be able to play on it.

"We had a right good choir for them days; the only
trouble was that everybody wanted to be leader. That's
a common failin' with church choirs, I've noticed.
Milly Amos sung soprano, and my Jane was the alto;
John Petty sung bass, and young Sam Crawford tenor;
and as for Uncle Jim Matthews, he sung everything,
and a plenty of it, too. Milly Amos used to say he
was worse'n a flea. He'd start out on the bass, and
first thing you knew he'd be singin' tenor with Sam

Crawford; and by the time Sam was good and mad, he'd be off onto the alto or the soprano. He was one o' these meddlesome old creeturs that thinks the world never moved till they got into it, and they've got to help everybody out with whatever they happen to be doin'. You've heard o' children bein' born kickin'. Well, Uncle Jim must 'a' been born singin'. I've seen people that said they didn't like the idea o' goin' to heaven and standin' around a throne and singin' hymns for ever and ever; but you couldn't 'a' pleased Uncle Jim better than to set him down in jest that sort o' heaven. Wherever there was a chance to get in some singin', there you'd be sure to find Uncle Jim. Folks used to say he enjoyed a funeral a heap better than he did a weddin', 'cause he could sing at the funeral, and he' couldn't at the weddin'; and Sam Crawford said he believed if Gabriel was to come down and blow his trumpet, Uncle Jim would git up and begin to sing.

"It wouldn't 'a' been so bad if he'd had any sort of a voice; but he'd been singin' all his life and hollerin' at protracted meetin's ever since he got religion, till he'd sung and hollered all the music out of his voice, and there wasn't much left but the old creaky machinery. It used to make me think of an old rickety

house with the blinds flappin' in the wind. It mortified us terrible to have any of the Methodists or Babtists come to our church. We was sort o' used to the
old man's capers, but people that wasn't couldn't keep
a straight face when the singin' begun, and it took
more grace than any of us had to keep from gittin' mad
when we seen people from another church laughin' at
our choir.

"The Babtists had a powerful protracted meetin'
one winter. Uncle Jim was there to help with the
singin', as a matter of course, and he begun to git
mightily interested in Babtist doctrines. Used to go
home with 'em after church and talk about Greek and
Hebrew words till the clock struck twelve. And one
communion Sunday he got up solemn as a ōwl and
marched out o' church jest before the bread and wine
was passed. Made out like he warn't sure he'd been
rightly babtized. The choir was mightily tickled at
the idea o' gittin' shed o' the old pest, and Sam Crawford went to him and told him he was on the right
track and to go ahead, for the Babtists was undoubtedly
correct, and if it wasn't for displeasin' his father and
mother he'd jine 'em himself. And then — Sam never
could let well enough alone — then he went to Bush

Elrod, the Babtist tenor, and says he, 'I hear you're goin' to have a new member in your choir.' And Bush says, 'Well, if the old idiot ever jines this church, we'll hold his head under the water so long that he won't be able to spile good music agin.' And then he give Uncle Jim a hint o' how things was; and when Uncle Jim heard that the Presbyterians was anxious to git shed of him, he found out right away that all them Greek and Hebrew words meant sprinklin' and infant babtism. So he settled down to stay where he was, and hollered louder'n ever the next Sunday.

"The old man was a good enough Christian, I reckon; but when it come to singin', he was a stumblin'-block and rock of offense to the whole church, and especially to the choir. The first thing Sally Ann said when she looked at the new organ was, 'Well, Jane, how do you reckon it's goin' to sound with Uncle Jim's voice?' and I laughed till I had to set down in a cheer.

"Well, when the men folks found out that our organ had come, they begun to wake up. Abram had brought it out Tuesday, and Wednesday night, as soon as prayer-meetin' broke, Parson Page says, says he:

'Brethren, there is a little business to be transacted. Please remain a few minutes longer.' And then, when we had set down agin, he went on to say that the sisters had raised money and bought an organ, and there was some division of opinion among the brethren about usin' it, so he would like to have the matter discussed. He used a lot o' big words and talked mighty smooth, and I knew there was trouble ahead for us women.

"Uncle Jim was the first one to speak. He was so anxious to begin, he could hardly wait for Parson Page to stop; and anybody would 'a' thought that he'd been up to heaven and talked with the Father and the Son and the Holy Ghost and all the angels, to hear him tell about the sort o' music there was in heaven, and the sort there ought to be on earth. 'Why, brethren,' says he, 'when John saw the heavens opened there wasn't no organs up there. God don't keer nothin',' says he, 'about such new-fangled, worldly instruments. But when a lot o' sweet human voices git to praisin' him, why, the very angels stop singin' to listen.'

"Milly Amos was right behind me, and she leaned over and says, 'Well, if the angels'd rather hear Uncle

41

Jim's singin' than our organ, they've got mighty pore taste, that's all I've got to say.'

"Silas Petty was the next one to git up, and says he: 'I never was in favor o' doin' things half-way, brethren; and if we've got to have the organ, why, we might as well have a monkey, too, and be done with it. For my part,' says he, 'I want to worship in the good old way my fathers and grandfathers worshiped in, and, unless my feelin's change very considerable, I shall have to withdraw from this church if any such Satan's music-box is set up in this holy place.'

"And Sally Ann turned around and whispered to me, 'We ought to 'a' got that organ long ago, Jane.' I like to 'a' laughed right out, and I leaned over, and .says I, 'Why don't you git up and talk for us, Sally Ann?' and she says: 'The spirit ain't moved me, Jane. I reckon it's too busy movin' Uncle Jim and Silas Petty.'

"Jest then I looked around, and there was Abram standin' up. Well, you could 'a' knocked me over with a feather. Abram always was one o' those close-mouthed men. Never spoke if he could git around it any way whatever. Parson Page used to git after him every protracted meetin' about not leadin' in prayer

42

and havin' family worship; but the spirit moved him that time sure, and there he was talkin' as glib as old Uncle Jim. And says he: 'Brethren, I'm not carin' much one way or another about this organ. I don't know how the angels feel about it, not havin' so much acquaintance with 'em as Uncle Jim has; but I do know enough about women to know that there ain't any use tryin' to stop 'em when they git their heads set on a thing, and I'm goin' to haul that organ over to-morrow mornin' and set it up for the choir to practise by Friday night. If I don't haul it over, Sally Ann and Jane'll tote it over between 'em, and if they can't put it into the church by the door, they'll hist a window and put it in that way. I reckon,' says he, 'I've got all the men against me in this matter, but then, I've got all the women on my side, and I reckon all the women and one man makes a pretty good majority, and so I'm goin' to haul the organ over to-morrow mornin'.'

"I declare I felt real proud of Abram, and I told him so that night when we was goin' home together. Then Parson Page he says, 'It seems to me there is sound sense in what Brother Parish says, and I suggest that we allow the sisters to have their way and give the organ a trial; and if we find that it is hurtful to the interests of the church, it will be an easy matter to remove it.' And Milly Amos says to me, 'I see 'em gittin' that organ out if we once git it in.'

"When the choir met Friday night, Milly come in all in a flurry, and says she: 'I hear Brother Gardner has gone to the 'Sociation down in Russellville, and all the Babtists are comin' to our church Sunday; and I want to show 'em what good music is this once, anyhow. Uncle Jim Matthews is laid up with rheumatism,' says she, 'and if that ain't a special providence I never saw one.' And Sam Crawford slapped his knee, and says he, 'Well, if the old man's rheumatism jest holds out over Sunday, them Babtists'll hear music sure.'

"Then Milly went on to tell that she'd been up to Squire Elrod's, and Miss Penelope, the squire's niece from Louisville, had promised to sing a voluntary Sunday.

"'Voluntary? What's that?' says Sam.

"'Why,' says Milly, 'it's a hymn that the choir, or somebody in it, sings of their own accord, without the preacher givin' it out; just like your tomatoes come up in the spring, voluntary, without you plantin' the seed. That's the way they do in the city churches,' says she, 'and we are goin' to put on city style Sunday.'

THE NEW ORGAN

"Then they went to work and practised some new tunes for the hymns Parson Page had give 'em, so if Uncle Jim's rheumatism didn't hold out, he'd still have to hold his peace.

"Well, Sunday come; but special providence was on Uncle Jim's side that time, and there he was as smilin' as a basket o' chips if he did have to walk with a cane. We'd had the church cleaned up as neat as a new pin. My Jane had put a bunch of honeysuckles and pinks on the organ, and everybody was dressed in their best. Miss Penelope was settin' at the organ with a bunch of roses in her hand, and the windows was all open, and you could see the trees wavin' in the wind and hear the birds singin' outside. I always did think that was the best part o' Sunday — that time jest before church begins."

Aunt Jane's voice dropped. Her words came slowly; and into the story fell one of those "flashes of silence" to which she was as little given as the great historian. The pan of dumplings waited for the sprinkling of spice and sugar, while she stood motionless, looking afar off, though her gaze apparently stopped on the vacant whitewashed wall before her. No mind reader's art was needed to tell what scene her faded eyes beheld.

There was the old church, with its battered furniture and high pulpit. For one brief moment the grave had yielded up its dead, and "the old familiar faces" looked out from every pew. We were very near together, Aunt Jane and I; but the breeze that fanned her brow was not the breeze I felt as I sat by her kitchen window. For her a wind was blowing across the plains of memory; and the honeysuckle odor it carried was not from the bush in the yard. It came, weighted with dreams, from the blossoms that her Jane had placed on the organ twenty-five years ago. A bob-white was calling in the meadow across the dusty road, and the echoes of the second bell had just died away. She and Abram were side by side in their accustomed place, and life lay like a watered garden in the peaceful stillness of the time "jest before church begins."

The asparagus on the stove boiled over with a great spluttering, and Aunt Jane came back to "the eternal now."

"Sakes alive!" she exclaimed, as she lifted the saucepan; "I must be gittin' old, to let things boil over this way while I'm studyin' about old times. I declare, I believe I've clean forgot what I was sayin'."

"You were at church," I suggested, "and the singing was about to begin."

"Sure enough! Well, all at once Miss Penelope laid her hands on the keys and begun to play and sing 'Nearer, My God, to Thee.' We'd heard that hymn all our lives at church and protracted meetin's and prayer-meetin's, but we didn't know how it could sound till Miss Penelope sung it all by herself that day with our new organ. I ricollect jest how she looked, pretty little thing that she was; and sometimes I can hear her voice jest as plain as I hear that robin out yonder in the ellum tree. Every word was jest like a bright new piece o' silver, and every note was jest like gold; and she was lookin' up through the winder at the trees and the sky like she was singin' to somebody we couldn't see. We clean forgot about the new organ and the Babtists; and I really believe we was feelin' nearer to God than we'd ever felt before. When she got through with the first verse, she played somethin' soft and sweet and begun again; and right in the middle of the first line — I declare, it's twenty-five years ago, but I git mad now when I think about it — right in the middle of the first line Uncle Jim jined in like an old squawkin' jay-bird, and sung like he was tryin' to drown out Miss Penelope and the new organ, too.

"Everybody give a jump when he first started, and he'd got nearly through the verse before we took in what was happenin'. Even the Babtists jest looked surprised like the rest of us. But when Miss Penelope begun the third time and Uncle Jim jined in with his hollerin', I saw Bush Elrod grin, and that grin spread all over the Babtist crowd in no time. The Presbyterian young folks was gigglin' behind their fans, and Bush got to laughin' till he had to git up and leave the church. They said he went up the road to Sam Amos' pasture and laid down on the ground and rolled over and over and laughed till he couldn't laugh any more.

"I was so mad I started to git up, though goodness knows what I could 'a' done. Abram he grabbed my dress and says, 'Steady, Jane!' jest like he was talkin' to the old mare. The thing that made me maddest was Silas Petty a-leanin' back in his pew and smilin' as satisfied as if he'd seen the salvation of the Lord. I didn't mind the Babtists half as much as I did Silas.

"The only person in the church that wasn't the least bit flustered was Miss Penelope. She was a Marshall on her mother's side, and I always said that nobody but a born lady could 'a' acted as she did. She sung right on as if everything was goin' exactly right and she'd been singin' hymns with Uncle Jim all her life. Two or three times when the old man kind o' lagged behind, it looked like she waited for him to ketch up, and when she got through and Uncle Jim was lumberin' on the last note, she folded her hands and set there lookin' out the winder where the sun was shinin' on the silver poplar trees, jest as peaceful as a angel, and the rest of us as mad as hornets. Milly Amos set back of Uncle Jim, and his red bandanna handkerchief was lyin' over his shoulders where he'd been shooin' the flies away. She told me the next day it was all she could do to keep from reachin' over and chokin' the old man off while Miss Penelope was singin'.

"I said Miss Penelope was the only one that wasn't flustered. I ought to 'a' said Miss Penelope and Uncle Jim. The old creetur was jest that simple-minded he didn't know he'd done anything out o' the way, and he set there lookin' as pleased as a child, and thinkin', I reckon, how smart he'd been to help Miss Penelope out with the singin'.

"The rest o' the hymns went off all right, and it did me good to see Uncle Jim's face when they struck up the new tunes. He tried to jine in, but he had to give it up and wait for the doxology.

"Parson Page preached a powerful good sermon, but I don't reckon it did some of us much good, we was so put out about Uncle Jim spilin' our voluntary.

"After meetin' broke and we was goin' home, me and Abram had to pass by Silas Petty's wagon. He was helpin' Maria in, and I don't know what she'd been sayin', but he says, 'It's a righteous judgment on you women, Maria, for profanin' the Lord's house with that there organ.' And, mad as I was, I had to laugh when I thought of old Uncle Jim Matthews executin' a judgment of the Lord. Uncle Jim never made more'n a half-way livin' at the carpenter's trade, and I reckon if the Lord had wanted anybody to help him execute a judgment, Uncle Jim would 'a' been the last man he'd 'a' thought of.

"Of course the choir was madder'n ever at Uncle Jim; and when Milly Amos had fever that summer, she called Sam to her the day she was at her worst, and pulled his head down and whispered as feeble as a baby: 'Don't let Uncle Jim sing at my funeral, Sam. I'll rise up out of my coffin if he does.' And Sam broke out a-laughin' and a-cryin' at the same time —

50

he thought a heap o' Milly — and says he, 'Well, Milly, if it'll have that effect, Uncle Jim shall sing at the funeral, sure.' And Milly got to laughin', weak as she was, and in a few minutes she dropped off to sleep, and when she woke up the fever was gone, and she begun to git well from that day. I always believed that laugh was the turnin'-p'int. Instead of Uncle Jim singin' at her funeral, she sung at Uncle Jim's, and broke down and cried like a child for all the mean things she'd said about the pore old creetur's voice."

The asparagus had been transferred to a china dish, and the browned butter was ready to pour over it. The potatoes were steaming themselves into mealy delicacy, and Aunt Jane peered into the stove where the dumplings were taking on a golden brown. Her story-telling evidently did not interfere with her culinary skill, and I said so.

"La, child," she replied, dashing a pinch of "seasonin'" into the peas, "when I git so old I can't do but one thing at a time, I'll try to die as soon as possible."

III

AUNT JANE'S ALBUM

III

AUNT JANE'S ALBUM

THEY were a bizarre mass of color on the sweet
spring landscape, those patchwork quilts, swaying in a long line under the elms and maples. The
old orchard made a blossoming background for them,
and farther off on the horizon rose the beauty of fresh
verdure and purple mist on those low hills, or "knobs,"
that are to the heart of the Kentuckian as the Alps
to the Swiss or the sea to the sailor.

I opened the gate softly and paused for a moment
between the blossoming lilacs that grew on each side
of the path. The fragrance of the white and the purple

blooms was like a resurrection-call over the graves of many a dead spring; and as I stood, shaken with thoughts as the flowers are with the winds, Aunt Jane came around from the back of the house, her black silk cape fluttering from her shoulders, and a calico sunbonnet hiding her features in its cavernous depth. She walked briskly to the clothes-line and began patting and smoothing the quilts where the breeze had disarranged them.

"Aunt Jane," I called out, "are you having a fair all by yourself?"

She turned quickly, pushing back the sunbonnet from her eyes.

"Why, child," she said, with a happy laugh, "you come pretty nigh skeerin' me. No, I ain't havin' any fair; I'm jest givin' my quilts their spring airin'. Twice a year I put 'em out in the sun and wind; and this mornin' the air smelt so sweet, I thought it was a good chance to freshen 'em up for the summer. It's about time to take 'em in now."

She began to fold the quilts and lay them over her arm, and I did the same. Back and forth we went from the clothes-line to the house, and from the house to the clothes-line, until the quilts were safely housed from the coming dewfall and piled on every available chair in the front room. I looked at them in sheer amazement. There seemed to be every pattern that the ingenuity of woman could devise and the industry of woman put together, — "four-patches," "nine-patches," "log-cabins," "wild-goose chases," "rising suns," hexagons, diamonds, and only Aunt Jane knows what else. As for color, a Sandwich Islander would have danced with joy at the sight of those reds, purples, yellows, and greens.

"Did you really make all these quilts, Aunt Jane?" I asked wonderingly.

Aunt Jane's eyes sparkled with pride.

"Every stitch of 'em, child," she said, "except the quiltin'. The neighbors used to come in and help some with that. I've heard folks say that piecin' quilts was nothin' but a waste o' time, but that ain't always so. They used to say that Sarah Jane Mitchell would set down right after breakfast and piece till it was time to git dinner, and then set and piece till she had to gif supper, and then piece by candle-light till she fell asleep in her cheer.

"I ricollect goin' over there one day, and Sarah Jane was gittin' dinner in a big hurry, for Sam had to go to town with some cattle, and there was a big basket o' quilt pieces in the middle o' the kitchen floor, and the house lookin' like a pigpen, and the children runnin' around half naked. And Sam he laughed, and says he, 'Aunt Jane, if we could wear quilts and eat quilts we'd be the richest people in the country.' Sam was the best-natured man that ever was, or he couldn't 'a' put up with Sarah Jane's shiftless ways. Hannah Crawford said she sent Sarah Jane a bundle o' caliker once by Sam, and Sam always declared he lost it. But Uncle Jim Matthews said he was ridin' along the road jest behind Sam, and he saw Sam throw it into the creek jest as he got on the bridge. I never blamed Sam a bit if he did.

"But there never was any time wasted on my quilts, child. I can look at every one of 'em with a clear conscience. I did my work faithful; and then, when I might 'a' set and held my hands, I'd make a block or two o' patchwork, and before long I'd have enough to put together in a quilt. I went to piecin' as soon as I was old enough to hold a needle and a piece o' cloth, and one o' the first things I can remember was settin' on the back door-step sewin' my quilt pieces, and mother praisin' my stitches. Nowadays folks don't have to sew unless they want to, but when I was a child there warn't any sewin'-machines, and it was about as needful for folks to know how to sew as it was for 'em to know how to eat; and every child that was well raised could hem and run and backstitch and gether and overhand by the time she was nine years old. Why, I'd pieced four quilts by the time I was nineteen years old, and when me and Abram set up housekeepin' I had bedclothes enough for three beds.

"I've had a heap o' comfort all my life makin' quilts, and now in my old age I wouldn't take a fortune for 'em. Set down here, child, where you can see out o' the winder and smell the lilacs, and we'll look at 'em all. You see, some folks has albums to put folks' pictures in to remember 'em by, and some folks has a book and writes down the things that happen every day so they won't forgit 'em; but, honey, these quilts is my albums and my di'ries, and whenever the weather's bad and I can't git out to see folks, I jest spread out my quilts and look at 'em and study over 'em, and it's jest like goin' back fifty or sixty years and livin' my life over agin.

"There ain't nothin' like a piece o' caliker for bringin' back old times, child, unless it's a flower or a bunch o' thyme or a piece o' pennyroy'l — anything that smells sweet. Why, I can go out yonder in the yard and gether a bunch o' that purple lilac and jest shut my eyes and see faces I ain't seen for fifty years, and somethin' goes through me like a flash o' lightnin', and it seems like I'm young agin jest for that minute."

Aunt Jane's hands were stroking lovingly a "ninepatch" that resembled the coat of many colors.

"Now this quilt, honey," she said, "I made out o' the pieces o' my children's clothes, their little dresses and waists and aprons. Some of 'em's dead, and some of 'em's grown and married and a long way off from me, further off than the ones that's dead, I sometimes think. But when I set down and look at this quilt and think over the pieces, it seems like they all come back, and I can see 'em playin' around the floors and goin' in and out, and hear 'em cryin' and laughin' and callin' me jest like they used to do before they grew up to men and women, and before there was any little graves o' mine out in the old buryin'-ground over yonder."

Wonderful imagination of motherhood that can bring childhood back from the dust of the grave and banish the wrinkles and gray hairs of age with no other talisman than a scrap of faded calico!

The old woman's hands were moving tremulously over the surface of the quilt as if they touched the golden curls of the little dream children who had vanished from her hearth so many years ago. But there were no tears either in her eyes or in her voice. I had long noticed that Aunt Jane always smiled when she spoke of the people whom the world calls "dead," or the things it calls "lost" or "past." These words seemed to have for her higher and tenderer meanings than are placed on them by the sorrowful heart of humanity.

But the moments were passing, and one could not dwell too long on any quilt, however well beloved. Aunt Jane rose briskly, folded up the one that lay across her knees, and whisked out another from the huge pile in an old splint-bottomed chair.

"Here's a piece o' one o' Sally Ann's purple caliker dresses. Sally Ann always thought a heap o' purple caliker. Here's one o' Milly Amos' ginghams — that pink-and-white one. And that piece o' white with the rosebuds in it, that's Miss Penelope's. She give it to me the summer before she died. Bless her soul! That dress jest matched her face exactly. Somehow her and her clothes always looked alike, and her voice matched her face, too. One o' the things I'm lookin' forward to, child, is seein' Miss Penelope agin and hearin' her sing. Voices and faces is alike; there's some that you can't remember, and there's some you can't forget. I've seen a heap o' people and heard a heap o' voices, but Miss Penelope's face was different from all the rest, and so was her voice. Why, if she said 'Good mornin'' to you, you'd hear that 'Good mornin' all day, and her singin' — I know there never was anything like it in this world. My grandchildren all laugh at me for thinkin' so much o' Miss Penelope's singin', but then they never heard her, and I have: that's the difference. My grandchild Henrietta was down here three or four years ago, and says she, 'Grandma, don't you want to go up to Louisville with me and hear Patti sing?' And says I, 'Patty who, child?' Says I, 'If it was to hear Miss Penelope sing, I'd carry these old bones o' mine clear from here to New York. But there ain't anybody else I want to hear sing bad enough to go up to Louisville or anywhere else. And some o' these days,' says I, '*I'm goin' to hear Miss Penelope sing.*'"

Aunt Jane laughed blithely, and it was impossible not to laugh with her.

"Honey," she said, in the next breath, lowering her voice and laying her finger on the rosebud piece, "honey, there's one thing I can't git over. Here's a piece o' Miss Penelope's dress, but *where's Miss Penelope?* Ain't it strange that a piece o' caliker'll outlast you and me? Don't it look like folks ought 'o hold on to their bodies as long as other folks holds on to a piece o' the dresses they used to wear?"

Questions as old as the human heart and its human grief! Here is the glove, but where is the hand it held but yesterday? Here the jewel that she wore, but where is she?

> "Where is the Pompadour now?
> *This* was the Pompadour's fan!"

Strange that such things as gloves, jewels, fans, and dresses can outlast a woman's form.

"Behold! I show you a mystery" — the mystery of mortality. And an eery feeling came over me as I entered into the old woman's mood and thought of the strong, vital bodies that had clothed themselves in those fabrics of purple and pink and white, and that now were dust and ashes lying in sad, neglected graves on farm and lonely roadside. There lay the quilt on our knees, and the gay scraps of calico seemed to mock us with their vivid colors. Aunt Jane's cheerful voice called me back from the tombs.

"Here's a piece o' one o' my dresses," she said; "brown ground with a red ring in it. Abram picked it out. And here's another one, that light yeller ground with the vine runnin' through it. I never had so many caliker dresses that I didn't want one more, for in my day folks used to think a caliker dress was good enough to wear anywhere. Abram knew my failin', and two or three times a year he'd bring me a dress when he come from town. And the dresses he'd pick out always suited me better'n the ones I picked.

"I ricollect I finished this quilt the summer before Mary Frances was born, and Sally Ann and Milly Amos and Maria Petty come over and give me a lift on the quiltin'. Here's Milly's work, here's Sally Ann's, and here's Maria's."

I looked, but my inexperienced eye could see no difference in the handiwork of the three women. Aunt Jane saw my look of incredulity.

"Now, child," she said, earnestly, "you think I'm foolin' you, but, la! there's jest as much difference in folks' sewin' as there is in their handwritin'. Milly made a fine stitch, but she couldn't keep on the line to save her life; Maria never could make a reg'lar stitch, some'd be long and some short, and Sally Ann's was reg'lar, but all of 'em coarse. I can see 'em now stoopin' over the quiltin' frames — Milly talkin' as hard as she sewed, Sally Ann throwin' in a word now and then, and Maria never openin' her mouth except to ask for the thread or the chalk. I ricollect they come over after dinner, and we got the quilt out o' the frames long before sundown, and the next day I begun bindin' it, and I got the premium on it that year at the Fair.

"I hardly ever showed a quilt at the Fair that I didn't take the premium, but here's one quilt that Sarah Jane Mitchell beat me on."

And Aunt Jane dragged out a ponderous, red-lined affair, the very antithesis of the silken, down-filled comfortable that rests so lightly on the couch of the modern dame.

"It makes me laugh jest to think o' that time, and how happy Sarah Jane was. It was way back yonder in the fifties. I ricollect we had a mighty fine Fair that year. The crops was all fine that season, and such apples and pears and grapes you never did see. The Floral Hall was full o' things, and the whole county turned out to go to the Fair. Abram and me got there the first day bright and early, and we was walkin' around the amp'itheater and lookin' at the townfolks and the sights, and we met Sally Ann. She stopped us, and says she, 'Sarah Jane Mitchell's got a quilt in the Floral Hall in competition with yours and Milly Amos'.' Says I, 'Is that all the competition there is?' And Sally Ann says, 'All that amounts to anything. There's one more, but it's about as bad a piece o' sewin' as Sarah Jane's, and that looks like it'd hardly hold together till the Fair's over. And,' says she, 'I don't believe there'll be any more. It looks like this was an off year on that particular kind o' quilt. I didn't get mine done,' says she, 'and neither did Maria Petty, and maybe it's a good thing after all.'

"Well, I saw in a minute what Sally Ann was aimin' at. And I says to Abram, 'Abram, haven't you got somethin' to do with app'intin' the judges for the women's things?' And he says, 'Yes.' And I says, 'Well, you see to it that Sally Ann gits app'inted to help judge the caliker quilts.' And bless your soul, Abram got me and Sally Ann both app'inted. The other judge was Mis' Doctor Brigham, one o' the town ladies. We told her all about what we wanted to do, and she jest laughed and says, 'Well, if that ain't the kindest, nicest thing! Of course we'll do it.'

"Seein' that I had a quilt there, I hadn't a bit o' business bein' a judge; but the first thing I did was to fold my quilt up and hide it under Maria Petty's big worsted quilt, and then we pinned the blue ribbon on Sarah Jane's and the red on Milly's. I'd fixed it all up with Milly, and she was jest as willin' as I was for Sarah Jane to have the premium. There was jest one thing I was afraid of: Milly was a good-hearted woman, but she never had much control over her tongue. And I says to her, says I: 'Milly, it's mighty good of you to give up your chance for the premium, but if Sarah Jane ever finds it out, that'll spoil everything. For,' says I, 'there ain't any kindness in doin' a person a favor and then tellin' everybody about it.' And Milly laughed, and says she: 'I know what you mean, Aunt Jane. It's mighty hard for me to keep from tellin' everything I know and some things I don't know, but,' says she, 'I'm never goin' to tell this, even to Sam.' And she kept her word, too. Every once in a while she'd come up to me and whisper, 'I ain't told it yet, Aunt Jane,' jest to see me laugh.

"As soon as the doors was open, after we'd all got

through judgin' and puttin' on the ribbons, Milly went and hunted Sarah Jane up and told her that her quilt had the blue ribbon. They said the pore thing like to 'a' fainted for joy. She turned right white, and had to lean up against the post for a while before she could git to the Floral Hall. I never shall forget her face. It was worth a dozen premiums to me, and Milly, too. She jest stood lookin' at that quilt and the blue ribbon on it, and her eyes was full o' tears and her lips quiverin', and then she started off and brought the children in to look at 'Mammy's quilt.' She met Sam on the way out, and says she: 'Sam, what do you reckon? My quilt took the premium.' And I believe in my soul Sam was as much pleased as Sarah Jane. He came saunterin' up, tryin' to look unconcerned, but anybody could see he was mighty well satisfied. It does a husband and wife a heap o' good to be proud of each other, and I reckon that was the first time Sam ever had cause to be proud o' pore Sarah Jane. It's my belief that he thought more o' Sarah Jane all the rest o' her life jest on account o' that premium. Me and Sally Ann helped her pick it out. She had her choice betwixt a butter-dish and a cup, and she took the cup. Folks used to laugh and say that that cup was the only thing in Sarah Jane's house that was kept clean and bright, and if it hadn't 'a' been solid silver, she'd 'a' wore it all out rubbin' it up. Sarah Jane died o' pneumonia about three or four years after that, and the folks that nursed her said she wouldn't take a drink o' water or a dose o' medicine out o' any cup but that. There's some folks, child, that don't have to do anything but walk along and hold out their hands, and the premiums jest naturally fall into 'em; and there's others that work and strive the best they know how, and nothin' ever seems to come to 'em; and I reckon nobody but the Lord and Sarah Jane knows how much happiness she got out o' that cup. I'm thankful she had that much pleasure before she died."

There was a quilt hanging over the foot of the bed that had about it a certain air of distinction. It was a solid mass of patchwork, composed of squares, parallelograms, and hexagons. The squares were of dark gray and red-brown, the hexagons were white, the parallelograms black and light gray. I felt sure that it had a history that set it apart from its ordinary fellows.

"Where did you get the pattern, Aunt Jane?" I asked. "I never saw anything like it."

The old lady's eyes sparkled, and she laughed with pure pleasure.

"That's what everybody says," she exclaimed, jumping up and spreading the favored quilt over two laden chairs, where its merits became more apparent and striking. "There ain't another quilt like this in the State o' Kentucky, or the world, for that matter. My granddaughter Henrietta, Mary Frances' youngest child, brought me this pattern *from Europe*."

She spoke the words as one might say, "from Paradise," or "from Olympus," or "from the Lost Atlantis." "Europe" was evidently a name to conjure with, a country of mystery and romance unspeakable. I had seen many things from many lands beyond the sea, but a quilt pattern from Europe! Here at last was something new under the sun. In what shop of London or Paris were quilt patterns kept on sale for the American tourist?

"You see," said Aunt Jane, "Henrietta married a mighty rich man, and jest as good as he's rich, too, and they went to Europe on their bridal trip. When she come home she brought me the prettiest shawl you ever saw. She made me stand up and shut my eyes, and she put it on my shoulders and made me look in

70

the lookin'-glass, and then she says, 'I brought you a new quilt pattern, too, grandma, and I want you to piece one quilt by it and leave it to me when you die.' And then she told me about goin' to a town over yonder they call Florence, and how she went into a big church that was built hundreds o' years before I was born. And she said the floor was made o' little pieces o' colored stone, all laid together in a pattern, and they called it mosaic. And says I, 'Honey, has it got anything to do with Moses and his law?' You know the Commandments was called the Mosaic Law, and was all on tables o' stone. And Henrietta jest laughed, and says she: 'No, grandma; I don't believe it has. But,' says she, 'the minute I stepped on that pavement I thought about you, and I drew this pattern off on a piece o' paper and brought it all the way to Kentucky for you to make a quilt by.' Henrietta bought the worsted for me, for she said it had to be jest the colors o' that pavement over yonder, and I made it that very winter."

Aunt Jane was regarding the quilt with worshipful eyes, and it really was an effective combination of color and form.

"Many a time while I was piecin' that," she said,

"I thought about the man that laid the pavement in that old church, and wondered what his name was, and how he looked, and what he'd think if he knew there was a old woman down here in Kentucky usin' his patterns to make a bedquilt."

It was indeed a far cry from the Florentine artisan of centuries ago to this humble worker in calico and worsted, but between the two stretched a cord of sympathy that made them one — the eternal aspiration after beauty.

"Honey," said Aunt Jane, suddenly, "did I ever show you my premiums?"

And then, with pleasant excitement in her manner, she arose, fumbled in her deep pocket for an ancient bunch of keys, and unlocked a cupboard on one side of the fireplace. One by one she drew them out, unrolled the soft yellow tissue-paper that enfolded them, and ranged them in a stately line on the old cherry center-table — nineteen sterling silver cups and goblets. "Abram took some of 'em on his fine stock, and I took some of 'em on my quilts and salt-risin' bread and cakes," she said, impressively.

To the artist his medals, to the soldier his cross of

the Legion of Honor, and to Aunt Jane her silver cups! All the triumph of a humble life was symbolized in these shining things. They were simple and genuine as the days in which they were made. A few of them boasted a beaded edge or a golden lining, but no engraving or embossing marred their silver purity. On the bottom of each was the stamp: "John B. Akin, Danville, Ky." There they stood,

"Filled to the brim with precious memories,"—

memories of the time when she and Abram had worked together in field or garden or home, and the County Fair brought to all a yearly opportunity to stand on the height of achievement and know somewhat the taste of Fame's enchanted cup.

"There's one for every child and every grandchild," she said, quietly, as she began wrapping them in the silky paper, and storing them carefully away in the cupboard, there to rest until the day when children and grandchildren would claim their own, and the treasures of the dead would come forth from the darkness to stand as heirlooms on fashionable sideboards and dam-ask-covered tables.

"Did you ever think, child," she said, presently,

73

"how much piecin' a quilt's like livin' a life? And as
for sermons, why, they ain't no better sermon to me
than a patchwork quilt, and the doctrines is right there
a heap plainer'n they are in the catechism. Many a
time I've set and listened to Parson Page preachin'
about predestination and free-will, and I've said to
myself, 'Well, I ain't never been through Centre
College up at Danville, but if I could jest git up in the
pulpit with one of my quilts, I could make it a heap
plainer to folks than parson's makin' it with all his big
words.' You see, you start out with jest so much caliker; you don't go to the store and pick it out and buy
it, but the neighbors will give you a piece here and a
piece there, and you'll have a piece left every time you
cut out a dress, and you take jest what happens to
come. And that's like predestination. But when it
comes to the cuttin' out, why, you're free to choose
your own pattern. You can give the same kind o'
pieces to two persons, and one'll make a 'nine-patch'
and one'll make a 'wild-goose chase,' and there'll be
two quilts made out o' the same kind o' pieces, and jest
as different as they can be. And that is jest the way
with livin'. The Lord sends us the pieces, but we can
cut 'em out and put 'em together pretty much to suit

ourselves, and there's a heap more in the cuttin' out and the sewin' than there is in the caliker. The same sort o' things comes into all lives, jest as the Apostle says, 'There hath no trouble taken you but is common to all men.'

"The same trouble'll come into two people's lives, and one'll take it and make one thing out of it, and the other'll make somethin' entirely different. There was Mary Harris and Mandy Crawford. They both lost their husbands the same year; and Mandy set down and cried and worried and wondered what on earth she was goin' to do, and the farm went to wrack and the children turned out bad, and she had to live with her son-in-law in her old age. But Mary, she got up and went to work, and made everybody about her work, too; and she managed the farm better'n it ever had been. managed before, and the boys all come up steady, hard-workin' men, and there wasn't a woman in the county better fixed up than Mary Harris. Things is predestined to come to us, honey, but we're jest as free as air to make what we please out of 'em. And when it comes to puttin' the pieces together, there's another time when we're free. You don't trust to luck for the caliker to put your quilt together with; you go to the store and pick it out yourself, any color you like. There's folks that always looks on the bright side and makes the best of everything, and that's like puttin' your quilt together with blue or pink or white or some other pretty color; and there's folks that never see anything but the dark side, and always lookin' for trouble, and treasurin' it up after they git it, and they're puttin' their lives together with black, jest like you would put a quilt together with some dark, ugly color. You can spoil the prettiest quilt pieces that ever was made jest by puttin' 'em together with the wrong color, and the best sort o' life is miserable if you don't look at things right and think about 'em right.

"Then there's another thing. I've seen folks piece and piece, but when it come to puttin' the blocks together and quiltin' and linin' it, they'd give out; and that's like folks that do a little here and a little there, but their lives ain't of much use after all, any more'n a lot o' loose pieces o' patchwork. And then while you're livin' your life, it looks pretty much like a jumble o' quilt pieces before they're put together; but when you git through with it, or pretty nigh through, as I am now, you'll see the use and the purpose of everything in it. Everything'll be in its right place jest like the squares in this 'four-patch,' and one piece may be pretty and another one ugly, but it all looks right when you see it finished and joined together."

Did I say that every pattern was represented? No, there was one notable omission. Not a single "crazy quilt" was there in the collection. I called Aunt Jane's attention to this lack.

"Child," she said, "I used to say there wasn't anything I couldn't do if I made up my mind to it. But I hadn't seen a 'crazy quilt' then. The first one I ever seen was up at Danville at Mary Frances', and Henrietta says, 'Now, grandma, you've got to make a crazy quilt; you've made every other sort that ever was heard of.' And she brought me the pieces and showed me how to baste 'em on the square, and said she'd work the fancy stitches around 'em for me. Well, I set there all the mornin' tryin' to fix up that square, and the more I tried, the uglier and crookeder the thing looked. And finally I says: 'Here, child, take your pieces. If I was to make this the way you want me to, they'd be a crazy quilt and a crazy woman, too.'"

Aunt Jane was laying the folded quilts in neat piles here and there about the room. There was a look of unspeakable satisfaction on her face — the look of the creator who sees his completed work and pronounces it good.

"I've been a hard worker all my life," she said, seating herself and folding her hands restfully, "but 'most all my work has been the kind that 'perishes with the usin',' as the Bible says. That's the discouragin' thing about a woman's work. Milly Amos used to say that if a woman was to see all the dishes that she had to wash before she died, piled up before her in one pile, she'd lie down and die right then and there. I've always had the name o' bein' a good housekeeper, but when I'm dead and gone there ain't anybody goin' to think o' the floors I've swept, and the tables I've scrubbed, and the old clothes I've patched, and the stockin's I've darned. Abram might 'a' remembered it, but he ain't here. But when one o' my grandchildren or great-grandchildren sees one o' these quilts, they'll think about Aunt Jane, and, wherever I am then, I'll know I ain't forgotten.

"I reckon everybody wants to leave somethin' behind that'll last after they're dead and gone. It don't look like it's worth while to live unless you can do that. The Bible says folks 'rest from their labors, and their works do follow them,' but that ain't so. They go, and

78

maybe they do rest, but their works stay right here, unless they're the sort that don't outlast the usin'. Now, some folks has money to build monuments with — great, tall, marble pillars, with angels on top of 'em, like you see in Cave Hill and them big city buryin'-grounds. And some folks can build churches and schools and hospitals to keep folks in mind of 'em, but all the work I've got to leave behind me is jest these quilts, and sometimes, when I'm settin' here, workin' with my caliker and gingham pieces, I'll finish off a block, and I laugh and say to myself, 'Well, here's another stone for the monument.'

"I reckon you think, child, that a caliker or a worsted quilt is a curious sort of a monument — 'bout as perishable as the sweepin' and scrubbin' and mendin'. But if folks values things rightly, and knows how to take care of 'em, there ain't many things that'll last longer'n a quilt. Why, I've got a blue and white counterpane that my mother's mother spun and wove, and there ain't a sign o' givin' out in it yet. I'm goin' to will that to my granddaughter that lives in Danville, Mary Frances' oldest child. She was down here last summer, and I was lookin' over my things and packin' 'em away, and she happened to see that counterpane, and says she, 'Grandma, I want you to will me that.' And says I: 'What do you want with that old thing, honey? You know you wouldn't sleep under such a counterpane as that.' And says she, 'No, but I'd hang it up over my parlor door for a —"

"Portière?" I suggested, as Aunt Jane hesitated for the unaccustomed word.

"That's it, child. Somehow I can't ricollect these new-fangled words, any more'n I can understand these new-fangled ways. Who'd ever 'a' thought that folks'd go to stringin' up bed-coverin's in their doors? And says I to Janie, 'You can hang your great-grand-mother's counterpane up in your parlor door if you want to, but,' says I, 'don't you ever make a door-curtain out o' one o' my quilts.' But la! the way things turn around, if I was to come back fifty years from now, like as not I'd find 'em usin' my quilts for window-curtains or door-mats."

We both laughed, and there rose in my mind a picture of a twentieth-century house decorated with Aunt Jane's "nine-patches" and "rising suns." How could the dear old woman know that the same esthetic sense that had drawn from their obscurity the white and blue counterpanes of colonial days would forever protect her loved quilts from such a desecration as she feared? As she lifted a pair of quilts from a chair near by, I caught sight of a pure white spread in striking contrast with the many-hued patchwork.

"Where did you get that Marseilles spread, Aunt Jane?" I asked, pointing to it. Aunt Jane lifted it and laid it on my lap without a word. Evidently she thought that here was something that could speak for itself. It was two layers of snowy cotton cloth thinly lined with cotton, and elaborately quilted into a perfect imitation of a Marseilles counterpane. The pattern was a tracery of roses, buds, and leaves, very much conventionalized, but still recognizable for the things they were. The stitches were fairylike, and altogether it might have covered the bed of a queen.

"I made every stitch o' that spread the year before me and Abram was married," she said. "I put it on my bed when we went to housekeepin'; it was on the bed when Abram died, and when I die I want 'em to cover me with it." There was a life-history in the simple words. I thought of Desdemona and her bridal sheets, and I did not offer to help Aunt Jane as she folded this quilt.

"I reckon you think," she resumed presently, "that

I'm a mean, stingy old creetur not to give Janie the counterpane now, instead o' hoardin' it up, and all these quilts too, and keepin' folks waitin' for 'em till I die. But, honey, it ain't all selfishness. I'd give away my best dress or my best bonnet or an acre o' ground to anybody that needed 'em more'n I did; but these quilts — Why, it looks like my whole life was sewed up in 'em, and I ain't goin' to part with 'em while life lasts."

There was a ring of passionate eagerness in the old voice, and she fell to putting away her treasures as if the suggestion of losing them had made her fearful of their safety.

I looked again at the heap of quilts. An hour ago they had been patchwork, and nothing more. But now! The old woman's words had wrought a transformation in the homely mass of calico and silk and worsted. Patchwork? Ah, no! It was memory, imagination, history, biography, joy, sorrow, philosophy, religion, romance, realism, life, love, and death; and over all, like a halo, the love of the artist for his work and the soul's longing for earthly immortality.

No wonder the wrinkled fingers smoothed them as reverently as we handle the garments of the dead.

IV

"SWEET DAY OF REST"

IV

"SWEET DAY OF REST"

I WALKED slowly down the "big road" that Sunday afternoon — slowly, as befitted the scene and the season; for who would hurry over the path that summer has prepared for the feet of earth's tired pilgrims? It was the middle of June, and Nature lay a vision of beauty in her vesture of flowers, leaves, and blossoming grasses. The sandy road was a pleasant walking-place; and if one tired of that, the short, thick grass on either side held a fairy path fragrant with pennyroyal, that most virtuous of herbs. A tall hedge of Osage orange bordered each side of the road, shading the traveler from the heat of the sun, and furnishing a nesting-place for numberless small birds that twittered and chirped their joy in life and love and June. Occasionally a gap in the foliage revealed the placid beauty of corn, oats, and clover, stretching in broad expanse to the distant purple woods, with here and there a field of the cloth of gold — the fast-ripening wheat that waited the hand of the mower. Not only is it the traveler's manifest duty to walk slowly in the midst of such surroundings, but he will do well if now and then he sits down and dreams.

As I made the turn in the road and drew near Aunt Jane's house, I heard her voice, a high, sweet, quavering treble, like the notes of an ancient harpsichord. She was singing a hymn that suited the day and the hour:

> "Welcome, sweet day of rest,
> That saw the Lord arise,
> Welcome to this reviving breast,
> And these rejoicing eyes."

Mingling with the song I could hear the creak of her old splint-bottomed chair as she rocked gently to and fro. Song and creak ceased at once when she caught sight of me, and before I had opened the gate she was hospitably placing another chair on the porch and smiling a welcome.

"Come in, child, and set down," she exclaimed, moving the rocker so that I might have a good view of the bit of landscape that she knew I loved to look at.

"Pennyroy'l! Now, child, how did you know I love to smell that?" She crushed the bunch in her withered hands, buried her face in it and sat for a moment with closed eyes. "Lord! Lord!" she exclaimed, with deep-drawn breath, "if I could jest tell how that makes me feel! I been smellin' pennyroy'l all my life, and now, when I get hold of a piece of it, sometimes it makes me feel like a little child, and then again it brings up the time when I was a gyirl, and if I was to keep on settin' here and rubbin' this pennyroy'l in my hands, I believe my whole life'd come back to me. Honeysuckles and pinks and roses ain't any sweeter to me. Me and old Uncle Harvey Dean was jest alike about pennyroy'l. Many a time I've seen Uncle Harvey searchin' around in the fence corners in the early part o' May to see if the pennyroy'l was up yet, and in

pennyroy'l time you never saw the old man that he
didn't have a bunch of it somewheres about him.
Aunt Maria Dean used to say there was dried pennyroy'l in every pocket of his coat, and he used to put a
big bunch of it on his piller at night.   Sundays it looked
like Uncle Harvey couldn't enjoy the preachin' and the
singin' unless he had a sprig of it in his hand, and I
ricollect once seein' him git up durin' the first prayer
and tiptoe out o' church and come back with a handful o' pennyroy'l that he'd gethered across the road, and
he'd set and smell it and look as pleased as a child with
a piece o' candy."

"Piercing sweet" the breath of the crushed wayside
herb rose on the air.   I had a distinct vision of Uncle
Harvey Dean, and wondered if the fields of asphodel
might not yield him some small harvest of his much-
loved earthly plant, or if he might not be drawn earth-
ward in "pennyroy'l time."

"I was jest settin' here restin'," resumed Aunt Jane,
"and thinkin' about Milly Amos.   I reckon you heard
me singin' fit to scare the crows as you come along.
We used to call that Milly Amos' hymn, and I never
can hear it without thinkin' o' Milly."

"Why was it Milly Amos' hymn?" I asked.

"SWEET DAY OF REST"

Aunt Jane laughed blithely.

"La, child!" she said, "don't you ever git tired o' my yarns? Here it is Sunday, and you tryin' to git me started talkin'; and when I git started you know there ain't any tellin' when I'll stop. Come on and le's look at the gyarden; that's more fittin' for Sunday evenin' than tellin' yarns."

So together we went into the garden and marveled happily over the growth of the tasseling corn, the extraordinarily long runners on the young strawberry plants, the size of the green tomatoes, and all the rest of the miracles that sunshine and rain had wrought since my last visit.

The first man and the first woman were gardeners, and there is something wrong in any descendant of theirs who does not love a garden. He is lacking in a primal instinct. But Aunt Jane was in this respect a true daughter of Eve, a faithful co-worker with the sunshine, the winds, the rain, and all other forces of nature.

"What do you reckon folks'd do," she inquired, "if it wasn't for plantin'-time and growin'-time and harvest-time? I've heard folks say they was tired o' livin', but as long as there's a gyarden to be planted and looked after there's somethin' to live for. And unless there's gyardens in heaven I'm pretty certain I ain't goin' to be satisfied there."

But the charms of the garden could not divert me from the main theme, and when we were seated again on the front porch I returned to Milly Amos and her hymn.

"You know," I said, "that there isn't any more harm in talking about a thing on Sunday than there is in thinking about it." And Aunt Jane yielded to the force of my logic.

"I reckon you've heard me tell many a time about our choir," she began, smoothing out her black silk apron with fingers that evidently felt the need of knitting or some other form of familiar work. "John Petty was the bass, Sam Crawford the tenor, my Jane was the alto, and Milly Amos sung soprano. I reckon Milly might 'a' been called the leader of the choir; she was the sort o' woman that generally leads wherever she happens to be, and she had the strongest, finest voice in the whole congregation. All the parts appeared to depend on her, and it seemed like her voice jest carried the rest o' the voices along like one big river that takes up all the little rivers and carries 'em down to the ocean. I used to think about the difference between her voice and Miss Penelope's. Milly's was jest as clear and true as Miss Penelope's, and four or five times as strong, but I'd ruther hear one note o' Miss Penelope's than a whole song o' Milly's. Milly's was jest a voice, and Miss Penelope's was a voice and somethin' else besides, but what that somethin' was I never could say. However, Milly was the very one for a choir; she kind o' kept 'em all together and led 'em along, and we was mighty proud of our choir in them days. We always had a voluntary after we got our new organ, and I used to look forward to Sunday on account o' that voluntary. It used to sound so pretty to hear 'em begin singin' when everything was still and solemn, and I can never forgit the hymns they sung then — Sam and Milly and John and my Jane.

"But there was one Sunday when Milly didn't sing. Her and Sam come in late, and I knew the minute I set eyes on Milly that somethin' was the matter. Generally she was smilin' and bowin' to people all around, but this time she walked in and set the children down, and then set down herself without even lookin' at anybody, to say nothin' o' smilin' or speakin'. Well, when half-past ten come, my Jane began to play 'Wel-

91

come, sweet day of rest,' and all of 'em begun singin'
except Milly. She set there with her mouth tight shut,
and let the bass and tenor and alto have it all their own
way. I thought maybe she was out o' breath from
comin' in late and in a hurry, and I looked for her to
jine in, but she jest set there, lookin' straight ahead of
her; and when Sam passed her a hymn-book, she took
hold of it and shut it up and let it drop in her lap. And
there was the tenor and the bass and the alto doin' their
best, and everybody laughin', or tryin' to keep from
laughin'. I reckon if Uncle Jim Matthews had 'a'
been there, he'd 'a' took Milly's place and helped 'em
out, but Uncle Jim'd been in his grave more'n two
years. Sam looked like he'd go through the floor, he
was so mortified, and he kept lookin' around at Milly
as much as to say, 'Why don't you sing? Please sing,
Milly,' but Milly never opened her mouth.

"I'd about concluded Milly must have the sore
throat or somethin' like that, but when the first hymn
was give out, Milly started in and sung as loud as anybody; and when the doxology come around, Milly was
on hand again, and everybody was settin' there wonderin' why on earth Milly hadn't sung in the voluntary.
When church was out, I heard Sam invitin' Brother

"SWEET DAY OF REST"

Hendricks to go home and take dinner with him — Brother Hendricks'd preached for us that day — and they all drove off together before I'd had time to speak to Milly.

"But that week, when the Mite Society met, Milly was there bright and early; and when we'd all got fairly started with our sewin', and everybody was in a good-humor, Sally Ann says, says she: 'Milly, I want to know why you didn't sing in that voluntary Sunday. I reckon everybody here wants to know,' says she, 'but nobody but me's got the courage to ask you.'

"And Milly's face got as red as a beet, and she burst out laughin', and says she: 'I declare, I'm ashamed to tell you all. I reckon Satan himself must 'a' been in me last Sunday. You know,' says she, 'there's some days when everything goes wrong with a woman, and last Sunday was one o' them days. I got up early,' says she, 'and dressed the children and fed my chickens and strained the milk and washed up the milk things and got breakfast and washed the dishes and cleaned up the house and gethered the vegetables for dinner and washed the children's hands and faces and put their Sunday clothes on 'em, and jest as I was startin' to git myself ready for church,' says she, 'I happened to think

93

that I hadn't skimmed the milk for the next day's churnin'. So I went down to the spring-house and did the skimmin', and jest as I picked up the cream-jar to put it up on that shelf Sam built for me, my foot slipped,' says she, 'and down I come and skinned my elbow on the rock step, and broke the jar all to smash and spilled the cream all over creation, and there I was — four pounds o' butter and a fifty-cent jar gone, and my spring-house in such a mess that I ain't through cleanin' it yet, and my right arm as stiff as a poker ever since.'

"We all had to laugh at the way Milly told it; and Sally Ann says, 'Well, that was enough to make a saint mad.' 'Yes,' says Milly, 'and you all know I'm far from bein' a saint. However,' says she, 'I picked up the pieces and washed up the worst o' the cream, and then I went to the house to git myself ready for church, and before I could git there, I heard Sam hollerin' for me to come and sew a button on his shirt; one of 'em had come off while he was tryin' to button it. And when I got out my work-basket, the children had been playin' with it, and there wasn't a needle in it, and my thimble was gone, and I had to hunt up the apron I was makin' for little Sam and git a needle off that, and I run the needle into my finger, not havin' any thimble, and got a blood spot on the bosom o' the shirt. Then,' says she, 'before I could git my dress over my head, here come little Sam with his clothes all dirty where he'd fell down in the mud, and there I had him to dress again, and that made me madder still; and then, when I finally got out to the wagon,' says she, 'I rubbed my clean dress against the wheel, and that made me mad again; and the nearer we got to the church, the madder I was; and now,' says she, 'do you reckon after all I'd been through that mornin', and dinner ahead of me to git, and the children to look after all the evenin', do you reckon that I felt like settin' up there and singin' "Welcome, sweet day o' rest"?' Says she, 'I ain't seen any day o' rest since the day I married Sam, and I don't expect to see any till the day I die; and if Parson Page wants that hymn sung, let him git up a choir of old maids and old bachelors, for they're the only people that ever see any rest Sunday or any other day.'

"We all laughed, and said we didn't blame Milly a bit for not singin' that hymn; and then Milly said: 'I reckon I might as well tell you all the whole story. By the time church was over,' says she, 'I'd kind o' cooled off, but when I heard Sam askin' Brother Hendricks to go home and take dinner with him, that made me mad again; for I knew that meant a big dinner for me to cook, and I made up my mind then and there that I wouldn't cook a blessed thing, company or no company. Sam'd killed chickens the night before,' says she, 'and they was all dressed and ready, down in the spring-house; and the vegetables was right there on the back porch, but I never touched 'em,' says she. 'I happened to have some cold ham and cold mutton on hand — not much of either one — and I sliced 'em and put the ham in one end o' the big meat-dish and the mutton in the other, with a big bare place between, so's everybody could see that there wasn't enough of either one to go 'round; and then,' says she, 'I sliced up a loaf o' my salt-risin' bread and got out a bowl o' honey and a dish o' damson preserves, and then I went out on the porch and told Sam that dinner was ready.'

"I never shall forgit how we all laughed when Milly was tellin' it. 'You know, Aunt Jane,' says she, 'how quick a man gits up when you tell him dinner's ready. Well, Sam he jumps up, and says he, "Why, you're mighty smart to-day, Milly; I don't believe there's another woman in the county that could git a Sunday dinner this quick." And says he, "Walk out, Brother Hendricks, walk right out."'"

Here Aunt Jane paused to laugh again at the long-past scene that her words called up.

"Milly used to say that Sam's face changed quicker'n a flash o' lightnin' when he saw the table, and he dropped down in his cheer and forgot to ask Brother Hendricks to say grace. 'Why, Milly,' says he, 'where's the dinner? Where's them chickens I killed last night, and the potatoes and corn and butter-beans?' And Milly jest looked him square in the face, and says she, 'The chickens are in the spring-house and the vegetables out on the back porch, and,' says she, 'do you suppose I'm goin' to cook a hot dinner for you all on this "sweet day o' rest"?'"

Aunt Jane stopped again to laugh.

"That wasn't a polite way for anybody to talk at their own table," she resumed, "and some of us asked Milly what Brother Hendricks said. And Milly's face got as red as a beet again, and she says: 'Why, he behaved so nice, he made me feel right ashamed o' myself for actin' so mean. He jest reached over and helped himself to everything he could reach, and says he, "This dinner may not suit you, Brother

Amos, but it's plenty good for me, and jest the kind I'm used to at home." Says he, "I'd rather eat a cold dinner any time than have a woman toilin' over a hot stove for me."'' And when he said that, Milly up and told him why it was she didn't feel like gittin' a hot dinner, and why she didn't sing in the voluntary; and when she'd got through, he says, 'Well, Sister Amos, if I'd been through all you have this mornin' and then had to git up and give out such a hymn as "Welcome, sweet day o' rest," I believe I'd be mad enough to pitch the hymn-book and the Bible at the deacons and the elders.' And then he turns around to Sam, and says he, 'Did you ever think, Brother Amos, that there ain't a pleasure men enjoy that women don't have to suffer for it?' And Milly said that made her feel meaner'n ever; and when supper-time come, she lit the fire and got the best hot supper she could — fried chicken and waffles and hot soda-biscuits and coffee and goodness knows what else. Now wasn't that jest like a woman, to give in after she'd had her own way for a while and could 'a' kept on havin' it? Abram used to say that women and runaway horses was jest alike; the best way to manage 'em both was to give 'em the rein and let 'em go till they got tired, and they'll always stop before they do any mischief. Milly said that supper tickled Sam pretty near to death. Sam was always mighty proud o' Milly's cookin'.

"So that's how we come to call that hymn Milly Amos' hymn, and as long as Milly lived folks'd look at her and laugh whenever the preacher give out 'Welcome, sweet day o' rest.'"

The story was over. Aunt Jane folded her hands, and we both surrendered ourselves to happy silence. All the faint, sweet sounds that break the stillness of a Sunday in the country came to our ears in gentle symphony, — the lisp of the leaves, the chirp of young chickens lost in the mazes of billowy grass, and the rustle of the silver poplar that turned into a mass of molten silver whenever the breeze touched it.

"When you've lived as long as I have, child," said Aunt Jane presently, "you'll feel that you've lived in two worlds. A short life don't see many changes, but in eighty years you can see old things passin' away and new ones comin' on to take their place, and when I look back at the way Sunday used to be kept and the way it's kept now, it's jest like bein' in another world. I hear folks talkin' about how wicked the world's growin' and wishin' they could go back to the old times, but it looks like to me there's jest as much kindness and goodness in folks nowadays as there was when I was young; and as for keepin' Sunday, why, I've noticed all my life that the folks that's strictest about that ain't always the best Christians, and I reckon there's been more foolishness preached and talked about keepin' the Sabbath day holy than about any other one thing.

"I ricollect some fifty-odd years ago the town folks got to keepin' Sunday mighty strict. They hadn't had a preacher for a long time, and the church'd been takin' things easy, and finally they got a new preacher from down in Tennessee, and the first thing he did was to draw the lines around 'em close and tight about keepin' Sunday. Some o' the members had been in the habit o' havin' their wood chopped on Sunday. Well, as soon as the new preacher come, he said that Sunday wood-choppin' had to cease amongst his church-members or he'd have 'em up before the session. I ricollect old Judge Morgan swore he'd have his wood chopped any day that suited him. And he had a load o' wood carried down cellar, and the nigger man chopped all day long down in the cellar, and nobody ever would 'a' found it out, but pretty soon they got up a big revival that lasted three months and spread 'way out into the country, and bless your life, old Judge Morgan was one o' the first to be converted; and when he give in his experience, he told about the wood-choppin', and how he hoped to be forgiven for breakin' the Sabbath day.

"Well, of course us people out in the country wouldn't be outdone by the town folks, so Parson Page got up and preached on the Fourth Commandment and all about that pore man that was stoned to death for pickin' up a few sticks on the seventh day. And Sam Amos, he says after meetin' broke, says he, 'It's my opinion that that man was a industrious, enterprisin' feller that was probably pickin' up kindlin'-wood to make his wife a fire, and,' says he, 'if they wanted to stone anybody to death they better 'a' picked out some lazy, triflin' feller that didn't have energy enough to work Sunday or any other day.' Sam always would have his say, and nothin' pleased him better'n to talk back to the preachers and git the better of 'em in a argument. I ricollect us women talked that sermon over at the Mite Society, and Maria Petty says: 'I don't know but what it's a wrong thing to say, but it looks to me like that Commandment wasn't intended for anybody but them Israelites. It was mighty easy for them to keep the Sabbath day holy, but,' says she, 'the Lord don't rain down manna in my yard. And,' says she, 'men can stop plowin' and plantin' on Sunday, but they don't stop eatin', and as long as men have to eat on Sunday, women'll have to work.'

"And Sally Ann, she spoke up, and says she, 'That's so; and these very preachers that talk so much about keepin' the Sabbath day holy, they'll walk down out o' their pulpits and set down at some woman's table and eat fried chicken and hot biscuits and corn bread and five or six kinds o' vegetables, and never think about the work it took to git the dinner, to say nothin' o' the dish-washin' to come after.'

"There's one thing, child, that I never told to anybody but Abram; I reckon it was wicked, and I ought to be ashamed to own it, but" — here her voice fell to a confessional key—"I never did like Sunday till I begun to git old. And the way Sunday used to be kept, it looks to me like nobody could 'a' been expected to like it but old folks and lazy folks. You see, I never was one o' these folks that's born tired. I loved to work. I never had need of any more rest than I got every night when I slept, and I woke up every mornin' ready for the day's work. I hear folks prayin' for rest and wishin' for rest, but, honey, all my prayer was,

102

'Lord, give me work, and strength enough to do it.' And when a person looks at all the things there is to be done in this world, they won't feel like restin' when they ain't tired.

"Abram used to say he believed I tried to make work for myself Sunday and every other day; and I ricollect I used to be right glad when any o' the neighbors'd git sick on Sunday and send for me to help nurse 'em. Nursing the sick was a work o' necessity, and mercy, too. And then, child, the Lord don't ever rest. The Bible says He rested on the seventh day when He got through makin' the world, and I reckon that was rest enough for Him. For, jest look; everything goes on Sundays jest the same as week-days. The grass grows, and the sun shines, and the wind blows, and He does it all."

> " 'For still the Lord is Lord of might;
> In deeds, in deeds He takes delight,' "

I said.

"That's it," said Aunt Jane, delightedly. "There ain't any religion in restin' unless you're tired, and work's jest as holy in his sight as rest."

Our faces were turned toward the western sky, where the sun was sinking behind the amethystine hills.

The swallows were darting and twittering over our heads, a somber flock of blackbirds rose from a huge oak tree in the meadow across the road, and darkened the sky for a moment in their flight to the cedars that were their nightly resting place. Gradually the mist changed from amethyst to rose, and the poorest object shared in the transfiguration of the sunset hour.

Is it unmeaning chance that sets man's days, his dusty, common days, between the glories of the rising and the setting sun, and his life, his dusty, common life, between the two solemnities of birth and death? Bounded by the splendors of the morning and evening skies, what glory of thought and deed should each day hold! What celestial dreams and vitalizing sleep should fill our nights! For why should day be more magnificent than life?

As we watched in understanding silence, the enchantment slowly faded. The day of rest was over, a night of rest was at hand; and in the shadowy hour between the two hovered the benediction of that peace which "passeth all understanding."

V

MILLY BAKER'S BOY

.

V

MILLY BAKER'S BOY

IT was the last Monday in May, and a steady stream of wagons, carriages, and horseback riders had been pouring into town over the smooth, graveled pike.

Aunt Jane stood on her front porch, looking around and above with evident delight. This was her gala Monday; and if any thoughts of the County Court days of happier years were in her mind, they were not permitted to mar her enjoyment of the present. There were no waters of Marah near her spring of remembrance.

"Clear as a whistle!" she exclaimed, peering through the tendrils of a Virginia creeper at the sea of blue ether where fleecy white clouds were floating, driven eastward by the fresh spring wind. "Folks'll come home dry to-night; last time they was as wet as drowned rats. Yonder comes the Crawfords, and there's Jim Amos on horseback in front of 'em. How d'ye, Jim! And yonder comes Richard Elrod in his new carriage. Jest look at him! I do believe he grows younger and handsomer every day of his life."

A sweet-faced woman sat beside him, and two pretty girls were in the seat behind them. Bowing courteously to the old woman on the door-step, Richard Elrod looked every inch a king of the soil and a perfect specimen of the gentleman farmer of Kentucky.

"The richest man in the county," said Aunt Jane exultingly, as she followed the vanishing carriage with her keen gaze. "He went to the legislatur' last winter; the 'Hon. Richard Elrod' they call him now. And I can remember the time when he was jest Milly Baker's boy, and nothin' honorable about it, either."

There was a suggestion of a story in the words and in the look in Aunt Jane's eyes. What wonder that the tides of thought flowed back into the channel of old times on a day like this, when every passing face was a challenge to memory? It needed but a hint to bring forth the recollections that the sight of Richard Elrod had stirred to life. The high-back rocker and the basket of knitting were transferred to the porch; and with the beauty and the music of a spring morning around us I listened to the story of Milly Baker's boy.

"I hardly know jest where to begin," said Aunt Jane, wrinkling her forehead meditatively and adjusting her needles. "Tellin' a story is somethin' like windin' off a skein o' yarn. There's jest two ends to the skein, though, and if you can git hold o' the right one it's easy work. But there's so many ways o' beginning a story, and you never know which one leads straightest to the p'int. I wonder many a time how folks ever finds out where to begin when they set out to write a book. However, I reckon if I start with Dick Elrod I'll git through somehow or other.

"You asked me jest now who Richard Elrod was. He was the son o' Dick Elrod, and Dick was the son of Richard Elrod, the old Squire. It's curious how you'll name two boys Richard, and one of 'em will always be called Richard and the other'll be called Dick. No-body ever would 'a' thought o' callin' Squire Elrod 'Dick,' he was Richard from the day he was born till the day he died. But his son was nothin' but Dick all his life; Richard didn't seem to fit him somehow. And I've noticed that you can tell what sort of a man a boy's goin' to make jest by knowin' whether folks calls him Richard or Dick. I ain't sayin' that every Richard is a good man and every Dick a bad one. All I mean is that there's as much difference betwixt a 'Dick' and a 'Richard' as there is betwixt a roastin' ear and a peck o' corn meal. Both of 'em's corn, and both of 'em may be good, but they ain't the same thing by a long jump. There's been a Richard in the Elrod family as far back as you could track 'em; all of 'em good, steady, God-fearin' men till Dick come along. He was an only child, and of course that made a bad matter worse.

"There's some men that's born to git women into trouble, and Dick was one of 'em. Jest as handsome as a picture, and two years ahead o' his age when it come to size, and a way about him, from the time he put on pants, that showed jest what kind of a man he was cut out for. If the children was playin' 'Jinny, Put the

110

Kittle on,' Dick would git kissed ten times to any other boy's once; and if it was 'Drop the Handkerchief,' every little gyirl in the ring'd be droppin' it behind Dick to git him to run after her, and that was the only time Dick ever did any runnin'. All he had to do was jest to sit still, and the gyirls did the runnin'. It was that way all his life; and folks used to say there was jest one woman in the world that Dick couldn't make a fool of, and that was his cousin Penelope, the old Squire's brother's child. She used to come down to the Squire's pretty near every summer, and when Dick saw how high and mighty she was, he begun to lay himself out to make her come down jest where the other women was, not because he keered anything for her, — such men never keer for anybody but theirselves, — he jest couldn't stand it to have a woman around unless she was throwin' herself at his head or at his feet. But he couldn't do anything with his cousin Penelope. She naturally despised him, and he hated her. Next to Miss Penelope, the only girl that appeared to be anything like a match for Dick was Annie Crawford, Old Man Bob Crawford's daughter. Old Man Bob was one o' the kind that thinks that the more children they've got the bigger men they are. Always made me think of Abraham and the rest o' the old patriarchs to see him come walkin' into church with them nine young ones at his heels, makin' so much racket you couldn't hear the sermon. He was mighty proud of his sons; but after Bob was born he wanted a daughter; and when they all kept turnin' out boys, he got crazier and crazier for a gyirl. Annie wasn't born till he was past sixty, and he like to 'a' lost his senses with joy. It was harvestin' time, and he jest stopped work and set on his front porch, and every time anybody passed by he'd holler, 'Well; neighbor, it's a gal this time!' If I'd 'a' been in Ann 'Liza's place, I'd 'a' gagged him. But la! she thought everything he did was all right. It got to be a reg'lar joke with the neighbors to ask Old Man Bob how many children he had, and he'd give a big laugh and say, 'Ten, neighbor, and all of 'em gals but nine.'

"Well, of course Annie was bound to be spoiled, especially as her mother died when she was jest four years old. How Ann 'Liza ever stood Old Man Bob and them nine boys as long as she did was a mystery to everybody. Ann 'Liza had done her best to manage Annie, with Old Man Bob pullin' against her all the

time, but after she died Annie took the place and everything and everybody on it. Old Man Bob had raised
all his boys on spare-the-rod-and-spile-the-child principle, but when Annie come, he turned his back on
Solomon and give out that Annie mustn't be crossed
by anybody. Sam Amos asked him once how he come
to change his mind so about raisin' children, and Old
Man Bob said he was of the opinion that that text
ought to read, 'Spare the rod and spile the boy'; that
Solomon had too much regyard for women to want to
whip a gal child. If ever there was an old idiot he was
one; I mean Old Man Bob, not Solomon; though
Solomon wasn't as wise as he might 'a' been in some
things.

"Well, Annie was a headstrong, high-tempered
child to begin with; and havin' nobody to control her,
she got to be the worst young one, I reckon, in the State
o' Kentucky. I used to feel right sorry for her little
brothers. They couldn't keep a top or a ball or marble
or any plaything to save their lives. Annie would cry
for 'em jest for pure meanness, and whatever it was
that Annie cried for they had to give it up or git a
whippin'. She'd break up their rabbit-traps and their
bird-cages and the little wheelbarrers and wagons

they'd make, and they didn't have any peace at home, pore little motherless things. I ricollect one day little Jim come runnin' over to my house draggin' his wagon loaded up with all his playthings, his little saw and hammer and some nails the cyarpenters had give him when Old Man Bob had his new stable built, and says he, 'Aunt Jane, please let me keep my tools over here. Annie says she's goin' to throw 'em in the well, and pappy'll make me give 'em to her if she cries for 'em.' Them tools stayed at my house till Jim outgrowed 'em, and he and Henry, the other little one, used to come and stay by the hour playin' with my Abram.

"It was all Old Man Bob could do to git a housekeeper to stay with him when Annie got older. One spring she broke up all the hen nests and turkey nests on the farm, and they had to buy chickens all summer and turkeys all next winter. They used to tell how she stood and hollered for two hours one day because the housekeeper wouldn't let her put her hand into a kittle o' boilin' lye soap. It's my belief that she was all that kept Old Man Bob from marryin' again in less'n a year after Ann 'Liza died. He courted three or four widders and old maids round the neighborhood, but there

114

wasn't one of 'em that anxious to marry that she'd take
Old Man Bob with Annie thrown in. As soon as she
got old enough, Old Man Bob carried her with him
wherever he went. County Court days you'd see him
goin' along on his big gray mare with Annie behind
him, holdin' on to the sides of his coat with her little
fat hands, her sunbonnet fallin' off and her curls blowin'
all around her face, — like as not she hadn't had 'em
combed for a week, — and in the evenin' about sunset
here they'd come, Annie in front fast asleep, and Old
Man Bob holdin' her on one arm and guidin' his horse
with the other. Harvestin' times Annie'd be out in
the field settin' on a shock o' wheat and orderin' the
hands around same as if she was the overseer; and Old
Man Bob'd jest stand back and shake his sides laughin'
and say: 'That's right, honey. Make 'em move lively.
If it wasn't for you, pappy couldn't git his harvestin'
done.'

"Every fall and spring he'd go to town to buy clothes
for her, and people used to say the storekeepers laid in
a extry stock jest for Old Man Bob, and charged him
two or three prices for everything he bought. He'd
walk into Tom Baker's store with his saddle-bags on
his arm and holler out, 'Well, what you got to-day?

Trot out your silks and your satins, and remember that the best ain't good enough for my little gal.'

"When Annie was twelve years old he took her off to Bardstown to git her education. When he come to say good-bye to her, he cried and she cried, and it ended with him settin' down and stayin' three weeks in Bardstown, waitin' for Annie to git over her homesickness. Folks never did git through plaguin' him about goin' off to boardin' school, and as soon as Sam Crawford seen him he says, 'Well, Uncle Bob, when do you reckon you'll git your diploma?'

"I never shall forgit the first time Annie come home to spend her Christmas. The neighbors didn't have any peace o' their lives for Old Man Bob tellin' 'em how Annie had growed, and how there wasn't a gal in the state that could hold a candle to her. And Sunday he come walkin' in church with Annie hangin' on to his arm jest as proud and happy as if he'd got a new wife.

"Annie had improved wonderful. It wasn't jest her looks, for she always was as pretty as a picture, but she was as nice-mannered, well-behaved a gyirl as you'd want to see. There was jest as much difference betwixt her then and what she used to be as there is betwixt a tame fox and a wild one. Of course the wildness is all there, but it's kind o' covered up under a lot o' cute little tricks and ways; and that's the way it was with Annie. Squire Elrod's pew was jest across the aisle from Old Man Bob's, and I could see Dick watchin' her durin' church time. But Annie never looked one way nor the other. She set there with her hands folded and her eyes straight before her, and nobody ever would 'a' thought that she'd been ridin' horses bareback and climbin' eight-rail fences ever since she could walk, mighty near.

"When she come back from school in June it was the same thing over again, Old Man Bob braggin' on her and everybody sayin' how sweet and pretty she was. Dick began to wait on her right away, and before long folks was sayin' that they was made for each other, especially as their farms jined. That's a fool notion, but you can't git it out o' some people's heads.

"Things went on this way for two or three years, Annie goin' and comin' and gittin' prettier all the time, and Dick waitin' on her whenever she was at home and carryin' on between times with every gyirl in the neighborhood. At last she come home for good, and Dick dropped all the others in a hurry and set out in earnest to git Annie. Folks said he was mightily in love, but accordin' to my way o' thinkin' there wasn't any love about it. The long and the short of it was that Annie knew how to manage him, and the other gyirls didn't. They was always right there in the neighborhood, and it don't help a woman to be always under a man's nose. But Annie was here and there and everywhere, visitin' in town and in Louisville and bringin' the town folks and the city folks home with her, and havin' dances and picnics, and doin' all she could to make Dick jealous. And then I always believed that Annie was jest as crazy about Dick as the rest o' the gyirls, but she had sense enough not to let him know it. It's human nature, you know, to want things that's hard to git. Why, if fleas and mosquitoes was sceerce, folks would go to huntin' 'em and makin' a big fuss over 'em. Annie made herself hard to git, and that's why Dick wanted her instead o' Harriet Amos, that was jest as good lookin' and better in every other way than Annie was. Everybody was sayin' what a blessed thing it was, and now Dick would give up his wild ways and settle down and be a comfort to the Squire in his old age.

"Well, along in the spring, a year after Annie got through with school, Sally Ann come to me, and says she, 'Jane, I saw somethin' last night and it's been botherin' me ever since;' and she went on to say how she was goin' home about dusk, and how she'd seen Dick Elrod and little Milly Baker at the turn o' the lane that used to lead up to Milly's house. 'They was standin' under the wild cherry tree in the fence corner,' says she, 'and the elderberry bushes was so thick that I could jest see Dick's head and shoulders and the top o' Milly's head, but they looked to be mighty close together, and Dick was stoopin' over and whisperin' somethin' to her.'

"Well, that set me to thinkin', and I ricollected seein' Dick comin' down the lane one evenin' about sunset, and at the same time I'd caught sight o' Milly walkin' away in the opposite direction. Our Mite Society met that day, and Sally Ann and me had it up, and we all talked it over. It come out that every woman there had seen the same things we'd been seein', but nobody said anything about it as long as they wasn't certain. 'Somethin' ought to be done,' says Sally Ann; 'it'd be a shame to let that pore child go to destruction right before our eyes when a word might save her.

She's fatherless, and pretty near motherless, too,' says she.

"You see, the Bakers was tenants of old Squire Elrod's, and after Milly's father died o' consumption the old Squire jest let 'em live on the same as before. Mis' Elrod give 'em quiltin' and sewin' to do, and they had their little gyarden, and managed to git along well enough. Some folks called 'em pore white trash. They was pore enough, goodness knows, but they was clean and hard-workin', and that's two things that 'trash' never is. I used to hear that Milly's mother come of a good family, but she'd married beneath herself and got down in the world like folks always do when they're cast off by their own people. Milly had come up like a wild rose in a fence corner, and she was jest the kind of a girl to be fooled by a man like Dick, handsome and smooth talkin', with all the ways and manners that take women in. Em'ly Crawford used to say it made her feel like a queen jest to see Dick take his hat off to her. If men's manners matched their hearts, honey, this'd be a heap easier world for women. But whenever you see a man that's got good manners and a bad heart, you may know there's trouble ahead for some woman.

"Well, us women talked it over till dark come; and I reckon if we had app'inted a committee to look after Milly and Dick, somethin' might have been done. But everybody's business is nobody's business, and I thought Sally Ann would go to Milly and give her a word o' warnin', and Sally Ann thought I'd do it, and so it went, and nothin' was said or done at last; and before long it was all over the neighborhood that pore little Milly was in trouble."

Aunt Jane paused, took off her glasses and wiped them carefully on a corner of her gingham apron.

"Many's the time," she said slowly, "that I've laid awake till the chickens crowed, blamin' myself and wonderin' how far I was responsible for Milly's mishap. I've lived a long time since then, and I don't worry any more about such things. There's some things that's got to be; and when a person is all wore out tryin' to find out why this thing happened and why that thing didn't happen, he can jest throw himself back on the eternal decrees, and it's like layin' down on a good soft feather bed after you've done a hard day's work. The preachers'll tell you that every man is his brother's keeper, but 'tain't so. I ain't my brother's keeper, nor my sister's, neither. There's jest one person I've got to keep, and that's myself.

"The Bible says, 'A word spoken in due season, how good it is!' But when folks is in love there ain't any due season for speakin' warnin' words to 'em. There was Emmeline Amos: her father told her if she married Hal, he'd cut her name out o' the family Bible and leave her clear out o' his will. But that didn't hinder her. She went right on and married him, and lived to rue the day she did it. No, child, there's mighty little salvation by words for folks that's in love. I reckon if a word from me would 'a' saved Milly, the word would 'a' been given to me, and the season too, and as they wasn't, why I hadn't any call to blame myself.

"Abram and Sam Crawford did try to talk to Old Man Bob; but, la! you might as well 'a' talked to the east wind. All he said was, 'If Annie wants Dick Elrod, Annie shall have him.' That's what he'd been sayin' ever since Annie was born. Nobody said anything to Annie, for she was the sort o' girl who didn't care whose feelin's was tramped on, if she jest had her own way.

"So it went on, and the weddin' day was set, and nothin' was talked about but Annie's first-day dress and Annie's second-day dress, and how many ruffles she had on her petticoats, and what the lace on her nightgowns cost; and all the time there was pore Milly Baker cryin' her eyes out night and day, and us women gittin' up all our old baby clothes for Dick Elrod's unborn child.''

Aunt Jane dropped her knitting in her lap, and gazed across the fields as if she were seeking in the sunlit ether the faces of those who moved and spoke in her story. A farm wagon came lumbering through the stillness, and she gathered up the double thread of story and knitting and went on.

"Annie always said she was goin' to have such a weddin' as the county never had seen, and she kept her word. Old Man Bob had the house fixed up inside and out. They sent up to Louisville for the cakes and things, and the weddin' cake was three feet high. There was a solid gold ring in it, and the bridesmaids cut for it; and every gyirl there had a slice o' the bride's cake to carry home to dream on that night. Annie's weddin' dress was white satin so heavy it stood alone, so they said. And Old Man Bob had the whole neighborhood laughin', tellin' how many heifers and steers it took to pay for the lace around the neck of it.

"Annie and Dick was married in October about the time the leaves fell, and Milly's boy was born the last o' November. Lord! Lord! what a world this is! Old Man Bob wouldn't hear to Annie's leavin' him, so they stayed right on in the old home place. In them days folks didn't go a-lopin' all over creation as soon as they got married; they settled down to housekeepin' like sensible folks ought to do. Old Lady Elrod was as foolish over Dick as Old Man Bob was over Annie, and it was laid down beforehand that they was to spend half the time at Old Man Bob's and half the time at the Squire's, 'bout the worst thing they could 'a' done. The further a young couple can git from the old folks on both sides the better for everybody concerned. And besides, Annie wasn't the kind of a gyirl to git along with Dick's mother. A gyirl with the kind o' raisin' Annie'd had wasn't any fit daughter-in-law for a particular, high-steppin' woman like Old Lady Elrod.

"There was some people that expected a heap o' Dick after he married, but I never did. If a man can't be faithful to a woman before he marries her, he ain't likely to be faithful after he marries her. And shore enough the shine wasn't off o' Annie's weddin' clothes before Dick was back to his old ways, drinkin' and carryin' on with the women same as ever, and the first thing we knew, him and Annie had a big quarrel, and Old Man Bob had ordered him off the place. However, they made it up and went over to the old Squire's to live, and things went on well enough till Annie's baby was born. Dick had set his heart on havin' a boy, but it turned out a girl, and as soon as they told him, he never even asked how Annie was, but jest went out to the stable and saddled his horse and galloped off, and nobody seen him for two days. He needn't 'a' took on so, for the pore little thing didn't live but a week. Annie had convulsions over Dick's leavin' her that way, and the doctor said that was what killed the child. Annie never was the same after this. She grieved for her child and lost her good looks, and when she lost them, she lost Dick. It wasn't long before Dick was livin' with his father, and she with hers. At last he went out West; and in less than three years Annie died; and a good thing she did, for a more soured, disappointed woman couldn't 'a' been found anywhere.

"Well, all this time Milly Baker's baby was growin' in grace, you might say. And a finer child never was born. Milly had named him Richard, and nature had wrote his father's name all over him. He was the livin' image of Dick, all but the look in his eyes; that was Milly's. Milly worshiped him, and there was few children raised any carefuler and better than Milly Baker's boy; that was what we always called him. Milly was nothin' but a child herself when he was born, but all at once she appeared to turn to a woman; acted like one and looked like one. It ain't time, honey, that makes people old; it's experience. Some folks never git over bein' children, and some never has any childhood; and pore little Milly's was cut short by trouble. If she felt ashamed of herself or the child, nobody ever knew it. I never could tell whether it was lack of sense, or whether she jest looked at things different from the rest of us; but to see her walk in church holding little Richard by the hand, nobody ever would 'a' thought but what she was a lawful wife. No woman could 'a' behaved better'n she did, I'm bound to say. She got better lookin' all the time, but she was as steady and sober as if she'd been sixty years old. Parson Page said once that Milly Baker had more dignity than any woman, young or old, that he'd ever seen. It seems right queer to talk about dignity in a pore gyirl who'd made the misstep she'd made, but I reckon

126

it was jest that that made us all come to treat her as if she was as good as anybody. People can set their own price on 'emselves, I've noticed; and if they keep it set, folks'll come up to it. Milly didn't seem to think that she had done anything wrong; and when she brought little Richard up for baptism there wasn't a dry eye in the church; and when she joined the church herself there wasn't anybody mean enough to say a word against it, not even Silas Petty.

"Squire Elrod give her the cottage rent free after her mother died, and betwixt nursin' and doin' fine needlework she made a good livin' for herself and the boy.

"Little Richard was a child worth workin' for from the start. Tall and straight as a saplin', and carried himself like he owned the earth, even when he was a little feller. It looked like all the good blood on both sides had come out in him, and there wasn't a smarter, handsomer boy in the county. The old Squire thought a heap of him, and nothin' but his pride kept him from ownin' the child outright and treatin' him like he was his own flesh and blood. Richard had an old head on young shoulders, though he was as full o' life as any boy; and by the time he was grown the old Squire

127

trusted him with everything on the place and looked to him the same as if he'd been a settled man. After Old Lady Elrod died, he broke terrible fast, and folks used to say it was a pitiful sight to see him when he'd be watchin' Richard overseein' the hands and tendin' to things about the place. He'd lean on the fence, his hands tremblin' and his face workin', thinkin' about Dick and grievin' over him and wishin', I reckon, that Dick had been such a man as Milly's boy was.

"All these years nobody ever heard from Dick. Once in a while somebody'd come from town and say they'd seen somebody that had seen somebody else, and that somebody had seen Dick way out in California or Lord knows where, and that was all the news that ever come back. We'd all jest about made up our minds that he was dead, when one mornin', along in corn-plantin' time, the news was brought and spread over the neighborhood in no time that Dick Elrod had come home and was lyin' at the p'int of death. I remembered hearin' a hack go by on the pike the night before, and wondered to myself what was up. I thought, maybe, it was a runaway couple or some such matter, but it was pore Dick comin' back to his father's house, like the Prodigal Son, after twenty years. It takes some folks a long time, child, to git tired of the swine and the husks.

"Well, of course, it made a big commotion, and before we'd hardly taken it in, we heard that he'd sent for Milly, and her and Richard had gone together up to the big house.

"Jane Ann Petty was keepin' house for the old Squire, and she told us afterwards how it all come about.

"We had a young probationer preachin' for us that summer, and as soon as he heard about Dick, he goes up to the big house without bein' sent for to talk to him about his soul. I reckon he thought it'd be a feather in his cap if he could convert a hardened sinner like Dick.

"Jane Ann said they took him into Dick's room, and he set down by the bed and begun to lay off the plan o' salvation jest like he was preachin' from the pulpit, and Dick listened and never took his eyes off his face. When he got through Dick says, says he:

"'Do you mean to say that all I've got to do to keep out of hell and get into heaven is to believe on the Lord Jesus Christ?' And Brother Jonas, he says:

"'Yes, my dear brother, "Believe on the Lord Jesus Christ, and thou shalt be saved. The blood of Jesus Christ, his Son, cleanseth us from all sin."'

"And they said Dick jest laughed a curious sort o' laugh and says he:

"'It's a pretty God that'll make such a bargain as that!' And says he, 'I was born bad, I've lived bad, and I'm dyin' bad; but I ain't a coward nor a sneak, and I'm goin' to hell for my sins like a man. Like a man, do you hear me?'

"Jane Ann said the look in his eyes was awful; and the preacher turned white as a sheet. It was curious talk for a death-bed; but, when you come to think about it, it's reasonable enough. When a man's got hell in his heart, what good is it goin' to do him to git into heaven?"

"What, indeed?" I echoed, thinking how delightful it was that Aunt Jane and Omar Khayyam should be of one mind on this subject.

"When Dick said this the young preacher got up to go, but Dick called him back, and says he, 'I don't want any of your preachin' or prayin', but you stay here; there's another sort of a job for you to do.' And then he turned around to the old Squire and says, 'Send for Milly.'

"When we all heard that Milly'd been sent for, the first thing we thought was, 'How on earth is Milly goin'

130

to tell Richard all he's got to know?' I never used to think we was anything over and above the ordinary out in our neighborhood, but when I ricollect that Richard Elrod come up from a boy to a man without knowin' who his father was, it seems like we must 'a' known how to hold our tongues anyhow. There wasn't man, woman, or child that ever hinted to Milly Baker's boy that he wasn't like other children, and so it was natural for us to wonder how Milly was goin' to tell him. Well, it wasn't any of our business, and we never found out. All we ever did know was that Milly and Richard walked over to the big house together, and Richard held his head as high as ever.

"They said that Dick give a start when Milly come into the room. I reckon he expected to see the same little girl he'd fooled twenty years back, and when she come walkin' in it jest took him by surprise.

"'Why, Milly,' says he, 'is this you?'

"And he held out his hand, and she walked over to the bed and laid her hand in his. Folks that was there say it was a strange sight for any one that remembered what them two used to be. Her so gentle and sweet-lookin', and him all wore out with bad livin' and wasted to a shadder of what he used to be.

"I've seen the same thing, child, over and over again. Two people'll start out together, and after a while they'll git separated, or, maybe, they'll live together a lifetime, and when they git to the end o' fifteen or twenty or twenty-five years, one'll be jest where he was when they set out, and the other'll be 'way up and 'way on, and they're jest nothin' but strangers after all. That's the way it was with Milly and Dick. They'd been sweethearts, and there was the child; but the father'd gone his way and the mother'd gone hers, and now there was somethin' between 'em like that 'great gulf' the Bible tells about. Well, they said Dick looked up at Milly like a hungry man looks at bread, and at last he says:

"'I'm goin' to make an honest woman of you, Milly.'

"And Milly looked him in the eyes and said as gentle and easy as if she'd been talkin' to a sick child: 'I've always been an honest woman, Dick.'

"This kind o' took him back again, but he says, right earnest and pitiful, 'I want to marry you, Milly; don't refuse me. I want to do one decent thing before I die. I've come all the way from California just for this. Surely you'll feel better if you are my lawful wife.'

"And they said Milly thought a minute and then she says: 'I don't believe it makes any difference with me, Dick. I've been through the worst, and I'm used to it. But if it'll make it any easier for you, I'll marry you. And then there's my boy; maybe it will be better for him.'

"'Where's the boy?' says Dick; 'I want to see him.'

"So Milly went and called Richard in. And as soon as Dick saw him he raised up on his elbow, weak as he was, and hollered out so you could hear him in the next room.

"'Why,' says he, 'it's myself! It's myself! Stand off there where I can see you, boy! Why, you're the man I ought to have been and couldn't be. These lyin' doctors,' says he, 'tell me that I haven't got a day to live, but I'm goin' to live another lifetime in you!'

"And then he fell back, gaspin' for breath, and young Richard stood there in the middle o' the floor with his arms folded and his face lookin' like it was made of stone.

"As soon as Dick could speak, they said he pulled Milly down and whispered something to her, and she went over to the chair where his clothes was hangin' and

133

felt in the pocket of the vest and got a little pearl ring out. They said she shook like a leaf when she saw it. And Dick says: 'I took it away from you, Milly, twenty years ago, for fear you'd use it for evidence against me — scoundrel that I was; and now I'm goin' to put it on your finger again, and the parson shall marry us fair and square. I've got the license here under my pillow.' And Milly leaned over and lifted him and propped him up with the pillows, and the young parson said the ceremony over 'em, with Jane Ann and the old Squire for witnesses.

"As soon as the parson got through, Dick says: 'Boy, won't you shake hands with your father? I wouldn't ask you before.' But Richard never stirred. And Milly got up and went to him and laid her hand on his arm and says: 'My son, come and speak to your father.' And he walked up and took Dick's pore wasted hand in his strong one, and the old Squire set there and sobbed like a child. Jane Ann said he held on to Richard's hand and looked at him for a long time, and then he reached under the pillow and brought out a paper, and says he: 'It's my will; open it after I'm gone. I've squandered a lot o' money out West, but there's a plenty left, and that minin' stock'll make you a rich man. It's all yours and your mother's. I wish it was more,' says he, 'for you're a son that a king'd be proud of.'

"Them was about the last words he said. Dr. Pendleton said he wouldn't live through the night, and sure enough he begun to sink as soon as the young parson left, and he died the next mornin' about day-break. Jane Ann said jest before he died he opened his eyes and mumbled somethin', and Milly seemed to know what he wanted, for she reached over and put Richard's hand on hers and Dick's, and he breathed his last jest that way.

"Milly wouldn't let a soul touch the corpse, but her and Richard. She was a mighty good hand at layin' out the dead, and them two washed and shrouded the body and laid it in the coffin, and the next day at the funeral Milly walked on one side o' the old Squire and Richard on the other; and the old man leaned on Richard like he'd found a prop for his last days.

"I ain't much of a hand to believe in signs, but there was one thing the day of the buryin' that I shall always ricollect. It had been rainin' off and on all day, — a soft, misty sort o' rain that's good for growin' things, — but while they were fillin' up the grave and smoothin'

135

it off, the sun broke out over in the west, and when we turned around to leave the grave there was the brightest, prettiest rainbow you ever saw; and when Milly and Richard got into the old Squire's carriage and rode home with him, that rainbow was right in front of 'em all the way home. It didn't mean much for Milly and the Squire, but I couldn't help thinkin' it was a promise o' better things for Richard, and maybe a hope for pore Dick.

"Milly didn't live long after this. They found her dead in her bed one mornin'. The doctor said it was heart disease; but it's my belief that she jest died because she thought she could do Richard a better turn by dyin' than livin'. She'd lived for him twenty years and seen him come into his rights, and I reckon she thought her work was done. Dyin' for people is a heap easier'n livin' for 'em, anyhow.

"The old Squire didn't outlive Milly many years, and when he died Richard come into all the Elrod property. You've seen the Elrod place, ain't you, child? That white house with big pillars and porches in front of it. It's three miles further on the pike, and folks'll drive out there jest to look at it. I've heard 'em call it a 'colonial mansion,' or some such name as that. It was all run down when Richard come into possession of it, but now it's one o' the finest places in the whole state. That's the way it is with families: one generation'll tear down and another generation'll build up. Richard's buildin' up all that his father tore down, and I'm in hopes his work'll last for many a day."

Aunt Jane's voice ceased, and there was a long silence. The full harvest of the story-telling was over; but sometimes there was an aftermath to Aunt Jane's tale, and for this I waited. I looked at the field opposite where the long, verdant rows gave promise of the autumn reaping, and my thoughts were busy tracing backward every link in the chain of circumstance that stretched between Milly Baker's boy of forty years ago and the handsome, prosperous man I had seen that morning. Ah, a goodly tale and a goodly ending! Aunt Jane spoke at last, and her words were an echo of my thought.

"There's lots of satisfactory things in this world, child," she said, beaming at me over her spectacles with the smile of the optimist who is born, not made. "There's a satisfaction in roundin' off the toe of a stockin', like I'm doin' now, and knowin' that your

137

work's goin' to keep somebody's feet warm next winter. There's a satisfaction in bakin' a nice, light batch o' bread for the children to eat up. There's a satisfaction in settin' on the porch in the cool o' the evenin' and thinkin' o' the good day's work behind you, and another good day that's comin' to-morrow. This world ain't a vale o' tears unless you make it so on purpose. But of all the satisfactions I ever experienced, the most satisfyin' is to see people git their just deserts right here in this world. I don't blame David for bein' out o' patience when he saw the wicked flourishin' like a green bay tree.

"I never was any hand for puttin' things off, whether it's work or punishment; and I've never got my own consent to this way o' skeerin' people with a hell and wheedlin' 'em with a heaven way off yonder in the next world. I ain't as old as Methuselah, but I've lived long enough to find out a few things; and one of 'em is that if people don't die before their time, they'll git their heaven and their hell right here in this world. And whenever I feel like doubtin' the justice o' the Lord, I think o' Milly Baker's boy, and how he got everything that belonged to him, and he didn't have to die and go to heaven to git it either."

"'Though the mills of God grind slowly, yet they grind
exceeding small;
Though with patience He stands waiting, with exact-
ness grinds He all.'"

I quoted the lines musingly, watching meanwhile
their effect on Aunt Jane. Her eyes sparkled as her
quick brain took in the meaning of the poet's words.

"That's it!" she exclaimed, — "that's it! I don't
mind waitin' myself and seein' other folks wait, too,
a reasonable time, but I do like to see everybody,
sooner or later, git the grist that rightly belongs to 'em."

VI
THE BAPTIZING AT KITTLE CREEK

VI

THE BAPTIZING AT KITTLE CREEK

"THERE'S a heap o' reasons for folks marryin'," said Aunt Jane, reflectively. "Some marries for love, some for money, some for a home; some marries jest to spite somebody else, and some, it looks like, marries for nothin' on earth but to have somebody always around to quarrel with about religion. That's the way it was with Marthy and Amos Matthews. I don't reckon you ever heard o' Marthy and Amos, did you, child? It's been many a year since I thought of 'em myself. But last Sunday evenin' I was over at Elnora Simpson's, and old Uncle Sam Simpson was there visitin'. Uncle Sam used to live in the neighborhood o' Goshen, but he moved up to Edmonson County way back yonder, I can't tell when, and every now and then he comes back to see his grandchildren. He's gittin' well on towards ninety, and I'm thinkin' this is about the last trip the old man'll make till he goes on his long journey. I was mighty glad to see him, and me and him set and talked about old times till the sun went down. What he didn't remember I did, and what I didn't remember he did; and when we got through talkin', Elnora — that's his grandson's wife — says, 'Well, Uncle Sam, if I could jest take down everything you and Aunt Jane said to-day, I'd have a pretty good history of everybody that ever lived in this county.'

"Uncle Sam was the one that started the talk about Marthy and Amos. He'd been leanin' on his cane lookin' out o' the door at Elnora's twins playin' on the grass, and all at once he says, says he, 'Jane, do you ricollect the time they had the big babtizin' down at Kittle

144

Creek?' And he got to laughin', and I got to laughin', and we set there and cackled like a pair o' old fools, and nobody but us two seein' anything funny about it."

Aunt Jane's ready laugh began again at the mere remembrance of her former mirth. I kept discreetly silent, fearing to break the flow of reminiscence by some ill-timed question.

"Nobody ever could see," she continued, "how it was that Amos Matthews and Marthy Crawford ever come to marry, unless it was jest as I said, to have somebody always handy to quarrel with about their religion; and I used to think sometimes that Marthy and Amos got more pleasure that way than most folks git out o' prayin' and singin' and listenin' to preachin'. Amos was the strictest sort of a Presbyterian, and Marthy was a Babtist, and to hear them two jawin' and arguin' and bringin' up Scripture texts about predestination and infant babtism and close communion and immersion was enough to make a person wish there wasn't such a thing as churches and doctrines. Brother Rice asked Sam Amos once if Marthy and Amos Matthews was Christians. Brother Rice had come to help Parson Page carry on a meetin', and he was tryin' to find out who was the sinners and who was the Christians. And Sam says, 'No; my Lord! It takes all o' Marthy's time to be a Babtist and all o' Amos' to be a Presbyterian. They ain't got time to be Christians.'

"Some folks wondered how they ever got time to do any courtin', they was so busy wranglin' over babtism and election. And after Marthy had her weddin' clothes all made they come to a dead stop. Amos said he wouldn't feel like they was rightly married if they didn't have a Presbyterian minister to marry 'em, and Marthy said it wouldn't be marryin' to her if they didn't have a Babtist. I was over at Hannah Crawford's one day, and she says, says she, 'Jane, I've been savin' up my eggs and butter for a month to make Marthy's weddin' cake, and if her and Amos don't come to an understandin' soon, it'll all be a dead loss.' And Marthy says, 'Well, mother, I may not have any cake at my weddin', and I may not have any weddin', but one thing is certain: I'm not goin' to give up my principles.'

"And Hannah sort o' groaned — she hadn't had any easy time with Miles Crawford — and says she, 'You pore foolish child! Principles ain't the only thing a woman has to give up when she gits married.'

"I don't know whether they ever would 'a' come to an agreement if it hadn't been for Brother Morris. He was the Presidin' Elder from town, and a powerful hand for jokin' with folks. He happened to meet Amos one day about this time, and says he, 'Amos, I hear you and Miss Marthy can't decide betwixt Brother Page and Brother Gyardner. It'd be a pity,' says he, 'to have a good match sp'iled for such a little matter, and s'pose you compromise and have me to marry you.'

"And Amos says, 'I don't know but what that's the best thing that could be done. I'll see Marthy and let you know.' And, bless your life, they was married a week from that day. I went over and helped Hannah with the cake, and Brother Morris said as pretty a ceremony over 'em as any Presbyterian or Babtist could 'a' said.

"Well, the next Sunday everybody was on the lookout to see which church the bride and groom'd go to. Bush Elrod bet a dollar that Marthy'd have her way, and Sam Amos bet a dollar that they'd be at the Presbyterian church. Sam won the bet, and we was all right glad that Marthy'd had the grace to give up that one time, anyhow. Amos was powerful pleased havin' Marthy with him, and they sung out of the same hymn-book and looked real happy. It looked like they was startin' out right, and I thought to myself, 'Well, here's a good beginnin', anyhow.' But it happened to be communion Sunday, and of all the unlucky things that could 'a' happened for Marthy and Amos, that was about the unluckiest. I said then that if Parson Page had been a woman, he'd 'a' postponed that communion. But a man couldn't be expected to have much sense about such matters, so he goes ahead and gives out the hymn,

" 'Twas on that dark and dreadful day;'

and everybody in church was lookin' at Amos and Marthy and watchin' to see what she was goin' to do. While they was singin' the hymn the church-members got up and went forward to the front seats, and Amos went with 'em. That left Marthy all alone in the pew, and I couldn't help feelin' sorry for her. She tried to look unconcerned, but anybody could see she felt sort o' forsaken and left out, and folks all lookin', and some of 'em whisperin' and nudgin' each other. I knew jest exactly how Marthy felt. Abram said to me when we was on the way home that day, 'Jane, if I'd 'a' been in Amos' place, I believe I'd 'a' set still with Marthy.

148

Marthy'd come with him and it looks like he ought to 'a' stayed with her.' I reckon, though, that Amos thought he was doin' right, and maybe it's foolish in women to care about things like that. Sam Amos used to say that nobody but God Almighty, that made her, ever could tell what a woman wanted and what she didn't want; and I've thought many a time that since He made women, it's a pity He couldn't 'a' made men with a better understandin' o' women's ways.

"Maybe if Amos'd set still that day, things would 'a' been different with him and Marthy all their lives, and then again, maybe it didn't make any difference. It's hard to tell jest what makes things go wrong in this world and what makes 'em go right. It's a mighty little thing for a man to git up and leave his wife settin' alone in a pew for a few minutes, but then there's mighty few things in this life that ain't little, till you git to follerin' 'em up and seein' what they come to."

I thought of Pippa's song:

> "Say not a small event! Why 'small' ?
> Costs it more pain that this, ye call
> A great event, should come to pass,
> Than that? Untwine me from the mass
> Of deeds which make up life, one deed
> Power shall fall short in or exceed!"

And Aunt Jane went serenely on:

"Anyhow, it wasn't long till Amos was goin' to his church and Marthy to hers, and they kept that up the rest of their lives. Still, they might 'a' got along well enough this way, for married folks don't have to think alike about everything, but they was eternally arguin' about their church doctrines. If Amos grumbled about the weather, Marthy'd say, 'Ain't everything predestined? Warn't this drought app'inted before the foundation of the world? What's the sense in grumblin' over the decrees of God?' And it got so that if Amos wanted to grumble over anything, he had to git away from home first, and that must 'a' been mighty wearin' on him; for, as a rule, a man never does any grumblin' except at home; but pore Amos didn't have that privilege. Sam Amos used to say — Sam wasn't a church-member himself — that there was some advantages about bein' a Babtist after all; you did have to go under the water, but then you had the right to grumble. But if a man believed that everything was predestined before the foundations of the world, there wasn't any sense or reason in findin' fault with anything that happened. And he believed that he'd ruther jine the Babtist church than the Presbyterian, for he didn't see how he could

150

carry on his farm without complainin' about the weather and the crops and things in general.

"If Marthy and Amos'd been divided on anything but their churches, the children might 'a' brought 'em together; but every time a child was born matters got worse. Amos, of course, wanted 'em all babtized in infancy, and Marthy wanted 'em immersed when they j'ined the church, and so it went. Amos had his way about the first one, and I never shall forgit the day it was born. I went over to help wait on Marthy and the baby, and as soon as I got the little thing dressed, we called Amos in to see it. Now, Amos always took his religion mighty hard. It didn't seem to bring him any comfort or peace o' mind. I've heard people say they didn't see how Presbyterians ever could be happy; but la, child, it's jest as easy to be happy in one church as in another. It all depends on what doctrines you think the most about. Now you take election and justification and sanctification, and you can git plenty o' comfort out o' them. But Amos never seemed to think of anything but reprobation and eternal damnation. Them doctrines jest seemed to weigh on him night and day. He used to say many a time that he didn't know whether he had made his callin' and election sure or not, and I don't believe he thought that anybody else had made theirs sure, either. Abram used to say that Amos looked like he was carryin' the sins o' the world on his shoulders.

"'That day the baby was born I thought to myself, 'Well, here's somethin' that'll make Amos forgit about his callin' and election for once, anyhow;' and I wrapped the little feller up in his blanket and held him to the light, so his father could see him; and Amos looked at him like he was skeered, for a minute, and then he says, 'O Lord! I hope it ain't a reprobate.'

"Now jest think of a man lookin' down into a little new-born baby's face and talkin' about reprobates!

"Marthy heard what he said, and says she, 'Amos, are you goin' to have him babtized in infancy?'

"'Why, yes,' says Amos, 'of course I am.'

"And Marthy says, 'Well, hadn't you better wait until you find out whether he's a reprobate or not? If he's a reprobate, babtizin' ain't goin' to do him any good, and if he's elected he don't need to be babtized.'

"And I says, 'For goodness' sake, Marthy, you and Amos let the doctrines alone, or you'll throw yourself into a fever.' And I pushed a rockin'-chair up by the bed and I says, 'Here, Amos, you set here by your wife,

152

and both of you thank the Lord for givin' you such a fine child;' and I laid the baby in Amos' arms, and went out in the gyarden to look around and git some fresh air. I gethered a bunch o' honeysuckles to put on Marthy's table, and when I got back, Marthy and the baby was both asleep, and Amos looked as if he was beginnin' to have some little hopes of the child's salvation.

"Marthy named him John; and Sam Amos said he reckoned it was for John the Babtist. But it wasn't; it was for Marthy's twin brother that died when he was jest three months old. Twins run in the Crawford family. Amos had him babtized in infancy jest like he said he would, and such a hollerin' and squallin' never was heard in Goshen church. The next day Sally Ann says to me, says she, 'That child must 'a' been a Babtist, Jane; for he didn't appear to favor infant babtism.'

"Well, Marthy had her say-so about the next child — that one was a boy, too, and they named him Amos for his father — and young Amos wasn't babtized in infancy; he was 'laid aside for immersion,' as Sam Amos said. Then it was Amos' time to have his way, and so they went on till young Amos was about fifteen years old and Marthy got him converted and ready to be immersed. The Babtists had a big meetin' that spring, and there was a dozen or more converts to be babtized when it was over. We'd been havin' mighty pleasant weather that March; I ricollect me and Abram planted our potatoes the first week in March, and I would put in some peas. Abram said it was too early, and sure enough the frost got 'em when they was about two inches high. It turned off real cold about the last o' March; and when the day for the babtizin' come, there was a pretty keen east wind, and Kittle Creek was mighty high and muddy, owin' to the rains they'd had further up. There was some talk o' puttin' off the babtizin' till better weather, but Brother Gyardner, he says: 'The colder the water, the warmer your faith, brethren; Christ never put off any babtizin' on account of the weather.'

"Sam Amos asked him if he didn't reckon there was some difference between the climate o' Kentucky and the climate o' Palestine. Sam was always a great hand to joke with the preachers. But the way things went that day the weather didn't make much difference anyhow to young Sam.

"The whole neighborhood turned out Sunday evenin'

and went over to Kittle Creek to see the big babtizin'. Marthy and Amos and all the children was there, and Marthy looked like she'd had a big streak o' good luck. Sam Amos says to me, 'Well, Aunt Jane, Marthy's waited a long time, but she'll have her innin's now.'

"Bush Elrod was the first one to go under the water; and when two or three more had been babtized, it was young Amos' time. I saw Marthy pushin' him forward and beckonin' to Brother Gyardner like she couldn't wait any longer.

"Nobody never did know exactly how it happened. Some folks said that young Amos wasn't overly anxious to go under the water that cold day, ·and he kind o' slipped behind his father when he saw Brother Gyardner comin' towards him; and some went so fur as to say that Brother Gyardner was in the habit o' takin' a little spirits after a babtizin' to keep from takin' cold, and that time he'd taken it beforehand, and didn't know exactly what he was about. Anyhow, the first thing we knew Brother Gyardner had hold o' Amos himself, leadin' him towards the water. Amos was a timid sort o' man, easy flustered, and it looked like he lost his wits and his tongue too. He was kind o' pullin' back and lookin' round in a skeered way, and

Brother Gyardner he hollered out, 'Come right along, brother! I know jest how it is myself; the spirit is willin', but the flesh is weak.' The Babtists was shoutin' 'Glory Hallelujah!' and Uncle Jim Matthews begun to sing, 'On Jordan's stormy banks I stand,' and pretty near everybody j'ined in till you couldn't hear your ears. The rest of us was about as flustered as Amos. We knew in reason that Brother Gyardner was makin' a big mistake, but we jest stood there and let things go on, and no tellin' what might 'a' happened if it hadn't been for Sam Amos. Sam was a cool-headed man, and nothin' ever flustered him. As soon as he saw how things was goin', he set down on the bank and pulled off his boots; and jest as Brother Gyardner got into the middle o' the creek, here come Sam wadin' up behind 'em, and grabbed Amos by the shoulder and hollered out, 'You got the wrong man, parson! Here, Amos, take hold o' me.' And he give Amos a jerk that nearly made Brother Gyardner lose his footin', and him and Amos waded up to the shore and left Brother Gyardner standin' there in the middle o' the creek lookin' like he'd lost his job.

"Well, that put a stop to the singin' and the shoutin', and the way folks laughed was scandalous. They had to walk Amos home in a hurry to git his wet clothes off, and Uncle Jim Matthews and Old Man Bob Crawford went with him to rub him down. Amos was subject to bronchitis, anyhow. Marthy went on ahead of 'em in the wagon to have hot water and blankets ready. I'll give Marthy that credit; she appeared to forgit all about the babtizin' when Amos come up so wet and shiverin'. Sam couldn't git his boots on over his wet socks, and as he'd walked over to the creek, Silas Petty had to take him home in his spring wagon. Brother Gyardner all this time was lookin' round for young Amos, but he wasn't to be found high nor low, and that set folks to laughin' again, and so many havin' to leave, the babtizin' was clean broke up. Milly come up jest as Sam was gittin' into Old Man Bob's wagon, and says she, 'Well, Sam, you've ruined your Sunday pants this time.' And Sam says, 'Pants nothin'. The rest o' you all can save your Sunday pants if you want to, but this here's a free country, and I ain't goin' to stand by and see a man babtized against his will while I'm able to save him.' And if Sam'd saved Amos' life, instead o' jest savin' him from babtism, Amos couldn't 'a' been gratefuler. When Sam broke his arm the follerin' summer, Amos went over and set up with him at night, and let his own wheat stand while he harvested Sam's.

"Well, the next time the 'Sociation met, the Babtists had somethin' new to talk about. Old Brother Gyardner got up, and says he, 'Brethren, there's a question that's been botherin' me for some time, and I'd like to hear it discussed and git it settled, if possible;' and says he, 'If a man should be babtized accidentally, and against his will, would he be a Babtist? or would he not?' And they begun to argue it, and they had it up and down, and some was of one opinion and some of another. Brother Gyardner said he was inclined to think that babtism made a man a Babtist, but old Brother Bascom said if a man wasn't a Babtist in his heart, all the water in the sea wouldn't make him one. And Brother Gyardner said that was knockin' the props clean from under the Babtist faith. 'For,' says he, 'if bein' a Babtist in the heart makes a man a Babtist, then babtism ain't necessary to salvation, and if babtism ain't necessary, what becomes o' the Babtist church?'

"Somebody told Amos about the dispute they was havin' over his case, and Amos says, 'If them fool Babtists want that question settled, let 'em come to me.' Says he, 'My father and mother was Presbyterians,

and my grandfather and grandmother and great-grand-
father and great-grandmother on both sides; I was
sprinkled in infancy, and I j'ined the Presbyterian church
as soon as I come to the age of accountability, and if
you was to carry me over to Jerusalem and babtize me
in the river Jordan itself, I'd still be a Presbyterian.'"

Here Aunt Jane paused to laugh again. "There's
some things, child," she said, as she wiped her glasses,
"that people'll laugh over and then forgit; and there's
some things they never git over laughin' about. The
Kittle Creek babtizin' was one o' that kind. Old Man
Bob Crawford used to say he wouldn't 'a' took five
hundred dollars for that babtizin'. Old Man Bob was
the biggest laugher in the country; you could hear him
for pretty near half a mile when he got in a laughin'
way; and he used to say that whenever he felt like havin'
a good laugh, all he had to do was to think of Amos and
how he looked with Brother Gyardner leadin' him into
the water, and the Babtists a-singin' over him. Bush
Elrod was another one that never got over it. Every
time he'd see Amos he'd begin to sing, 'On Jordan's
stormy banks I stand,' and Amos couldn't git out o' the
way quick enough.

"Well, that's what made me and old Uncle Sam

Simpson laugh so last Sunday. I don't reckon there's anything funny in it to folks that never seen it; but when old people git together and call up old times, they can see jest how folks looked and acted, and it's like livin' it all over again."

"I don't believe you can see it any plainer than I do, Aunt Jane," I hastened to assure her. "It is all as clear to me as any picture I ever saw. It was in March, you say, and the wind was cool, but the sun was warm; and if you sat in a sheltered place you might almost think it was the last of April."

"That's so, child. I remember me and Abram set under the bank on a rock that kind o' cut off the north wind, and it was real pleasant."

"Then there must have been a purple haze on the hills; and, while the trees were still bare, there was a look about them as if the coming leaves were casting their shadows before. There were heaps of brown leaves from last year's autumn in the fence corners, and as you and Uncle Abram walked home, you looked under them to see if the violets were coming up, and found some tiny wood ferns."

Aunt Jane dropped her knitting and leaned back in the high old-fashioned chair.

"Why, child," she said in an awe-struck tone, "are you a fortune-teller?"

"Not at all, Aunt Jane," I said, laughing at the dear old lady's consternation. "I am only a good guesser; and I wanted you to know that I not only see the things that you see and tell me, but some of the things that you see and don't tell me. Did Marthy ever get young Amos baptized?" I asked.

"La, yes," laughed Aunt Jane. "They finished up the babtizin' two weeks after that. It was a nice, pleasant day, and young Amos went under the water all right; but mighty little good it did him after all. For as soon as he come of age, he married Matildy Harris (Matildy was a Methodist), and he got to goin' to church with his wife, and that was the last of his Babtist raisin'."

Then we both were silent for a while, and I watched the gathering thunder-clouds in the west. A low rumble of thunder broke the stillness of the August afternoon. Aunt Jane looked up apprehensively.

"There's goin' to be a storm betwixt now and sundown," she said, "but I reckon them young turkeys'll be safe under their mother's wings by that time."

"Don't you think a wife ought to join her husband's

161

church, Aunt Jane?" I asked with idle irrelevance to
her remark.

"Sometimes she ought and sometimes she oughtn't,"
replied Aunt Jane oracularly. "There ain't any rule
about it. Everybody's got to be their own judge about
such matters. If I'd 'a' been in Marthy's place, I
wouldn't 'a' j'ined Amos' church, and if I'd been in
Amos' place I wouldn't 'a' j'ined Marthy's church.
So there it is."

"But didn't you join Uncle Abram's church?" I
asked, in a laudable endeavor to get at the root of
the matter.

"Yes, I did," said Aunt Jane stoutly; "but that's
a mighty different thing. Of course, I went with
Abram, and if I had it to do over again, I'd do it. You
see the way of it was this: my folks was Campbellites,
or Christians they'd ruther be called. It's curious how
they don't like to be called Campbellites. Methodists
don't mind bein' called Wesleyans, and Presbyterians
don't git mad if you call 'em Calvinists, and I reckon
Alexander Campbell was jest as good a man as Wesley
and a sight better'n Calvin, but you can't make a
Campbellite madder than to call him a Campbellite.
However, as I was sayin', Alexander Campbell himself

babtized my father and mother out here in Drake's Creek, and I was brought up to think that my church was *the* Christian church, sure enough. But when me and Abram married, neither one of us was thinkin' much about churches. I used to tell Marthy that if a man'd come talkin' church to me, when he ought to been courtin' me, I'd 'a' told him to go on and marry a hymn-book or a catechism. I believe in religion jest as much as anybody, but a man that can't forgit his religion while he's courtin' a woman ain't worth havin'. That's my opinion. But as I was sayin', me and Abram had the church question to settle after we was married, and I don't believe either one of us thought about it till Sunday mornin' come. I ricollect it jest like it was yesterday. We was married in June, and you know how things always look about then. I've thought many a day, when I've been out in the gyarden workin' with my vegetables and getherin' my honeysuckles and roses, that if folks could jest live on and never git old and it'd stay June forever, that this world'd be heaven enough for anybody. And that's the way it was that Sunday mornin'. I ricollect I had on my 'second-day' dress, the prettiest sort of a change-able silk, kind 'o dove color and pink, and I had a leghorn bonnet on with pink roses inside the brim, and black lace mitts on my hands. I stood up before the glass jest before I went out to the gate where Abram was, waitin' for me, and I looked as pretty as a pink, if I do say it. 'Self-praise goes but a little ways,' my mother used to tell me, when I was a gyirl; but I reckon there ain't any harm in an old woman like me tellin' how she looked when she was a bride more'n sixty years ago."

And a faint color came into the wrinkled cheeks, while her clear, high laugh rang out. The outward symbols of youth and beauty were gone, but their unquenchable spirit lay warm under the ashes of nearly eight decades.

"Well, I went out, and Abram helped me into the buggy and, instead o' goin' straight on to Goshen church, he turned around and drove out to my church. When we walked in I could see folks nudgin' each other and laughin', and when meetin' broke and we was fixin' to go home, Aunt Maria Taylor grabbed hold o' me and pulled me off to one side and says she, 'That's right, Jane, you're beginnin' in time. Jest break a man in at the start, and you won't have no trouble afterwards.' And I jest laughed in her face and went on to where

Abram was waitin' for me. I was too happy to git mad that day. Well, the next Sunday, when we got into the buggy and Abram started to turn round, I took hold o' the reins and says I, 'It's my time to drive, Abram; you had your way last Sunday, and now I'm goin' to have mine.' And I snapped the whip over old Nell's back and drove right on to Goshen, and Abram jest set back and laughed fit to kill.

"We went on that way for two or three months, folks sayin' that Abram and Jane Parrish couldn't go to the same church two Sundays straight along to save their lives, and everybody wonderin' which of us'd have their way in the long run. And me and Abram jest laughed in our sleeves and paid no attention to 'em; for there never was but one way for us, anyhow, and that wasn't Abram's way nor my way; it was jest *our* way. There's lots of married folks, honey, and one of 'em's here and one of 'em's gone over yonder, and there's a long, deep grave between 'em; but they're a heap nearer to each other than two livin' people that stay in the same house, and eat at the same table, and sleep in the same bed, and all the time there's two great thick church walls between 'em and growin' thicker and higher every day. Sam Amos used to say that if religion made folks act like

Marthy and Amos did, he believed he'd ruther have less religion or none at all. But, honey, when you see married folks quarrelin' over their churches, it ain't too much religion that's the cause o' the trouble, it's too little love. Jest ricollect that; if folks love each other right, religion ain't goin' to come between 'em.

"Well, as soon as cold weather set in they started up a big revival at Goshen church. After the meetin' had been goin' on for three or four weeks, Parson Page give out one Sunday that the session would meet on the follerin' Thursday to examine all that had experienced a change o' heart and wanted to unite with the church. I never said a word to Abram, but Thursday evenin' while he was out on the farm mendin' some fences that the cattle had broke down, I harnessed old Nell to the buggy and drove out to Goshen. All the converts was there, and the session was questionin' and examinin' when I got in. When it come my turn, Parson Page begun askin' me if I'd made my callin' and election sure, and I come right out, and says I, 'I don't know much about callin' and election, Brother Page; I reckon I'm a Christian,' says I, 'for I've been tryin' to do right by everybody ever since I was old enough to know the difference betwixt right and wrong; but, if the plain truth was told, I'm j'inin' this church jest because it's Abram's church, and I want to please him. And that's all the testimony I've got to give.' And Parson Page put his hand over his mouth to keep from laughin' — he was a young man then and hadn't been married long himself — and says he, 'That'll do, Sister Parrish; brethren, we'll pass on to the next candidate.' I left 'em examinin' Sam Crawford about his callin' and election, and I got home before Abram come to the house, and the next day when I walked up with the rest of 'em Abram was the only person in the church that was surprised. When they'd got through givin' us the right hand o' fellowship, and I went back to our pew, Abram took hold o' my hand and held on to it like he never would let go, and I knew I'd done the right thing and I never would regret it."

There was a light on the old woman's face that made me turn my eyes away. Here was a personal revelation that should have satisfied the most exacting, but my vulgar curiosity cried out for further light on the past.

"What would you have done," I asked, "if Uncle Abram hadn't turned the horse that Sunday morning — if he had gone straight on to Goshen?"

Aunt Jane regarded me for a moment with a look of pitying allowance, such as one bestows on a child who doesn't know any better than to ask stupid questions.

"Shuh, child," she said with carcless brevity, "Abram couldn't 'a' done such a thing as that."

VII

HOW SAM AMOS RODE IN THE TOURNAMENT

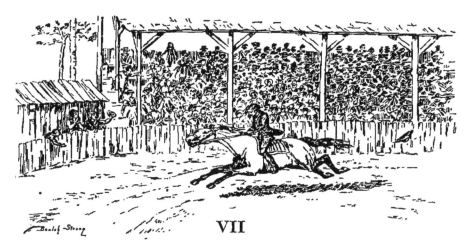

VII

HOW SAM AMOS RODE IN THE TOURNAMENT

"**T**HERE'S one thing I'd like mighty well to see again before I die," said Aunt Jane, "and that is a good, old-fashioned fair. The apostle says we must 'press forward, forgetting the things that are behind,' but there's some things I've left behind that I can't never forget, and the fairs we had in my day is one of 'em."

It was the quietest hour of an August afternoon — that time when one seems to have reached "the land where it is always afternoon" — and Aunt Jane and I were sitting on the back porch, shelling butter-beans for the next day's market. Before us lay the garden in the splendid fulness of late summer. Concord and Catawba grapes loaded the vines on the rickety old arbor; tomatoes were ripening in reckless plenty, to be given to the neighbors, or to lie in tempting rows on the window-sill of the kitchen and the shelves of the back porch; the second planting of cucumber vines ran in flowery luxuriance over the space allotted to them, and even encroached on the territory of the squashes and melons. Damsons hung purpling over the eaves of the house, and wasps and bees kept up a lively buzzing as they feasted on the windfalls of the old yellow peach tree near the garden gate. Nature had distributed her sunshine and showers with wise generosity that year, and neither in field nor in garden was there lack of any good thing. Perhaps it was this gracious abundance, presaging fine exhibits at the coming fair, that turned Aunt Jane's thoughts towards the fairs of her youth.

"Folks nowadays don't seem to think much about fairs," she continued; "but when I was young a fair was something that the grown folks looked forward to jest like children look for Christmas. The women and the men, too, was gittin' ready for the fair all the year round, the women piecin' quilts and knittin' socks and weavin' carpets and puttin' up preserves and pickles, and the men raisin' fine stock; and when the fair come, it was worth goin' to, child, and worth rememberin' after you'd gone to it.

"I hear folks talkin' about the fair every year, and I laugh to myself and I say, 'You folks don't know what a fair is.' And I set out there on my porch fair week and watch the buggies and wagons goin' by in the mornin' and comin' home at night, and I git right happy, thinkin' about the time when me and Abram and the children used to go over the same road to the fair, but a mighty different sort of fair from what they have nowadays. One thing is, honey, they have the fairs too soon. It never was intended for folks to go to fairs in hot weather, and here they've got to havin' 'em the first week in September, about the hottest, driest, dustiest time of the whole year. Nothin' looks pretty then, and it always makes me think o' folks when they've been wearin' their summer clothes for three months, and everything's all faded and dusty and drabbled. That's the way it generally is in September. But jest wait till two or three good rains come, and everything's washed clean and sweet, and the trees look like they'd got a new set o' leaves, and the grass comes out green and fresh like it does in the spring, and the nights and the mornin's feel cool, though it's hot enough in the middle o' the day; and maybe there'll come a touch of early frost, jest enough to turn the top leaves on the sugar maples. That's October, child, and that's the time for a fair.

"Lord, the good times I've seen in them days! Startin' early and comin' home late, with the sun settin' in front of you, and by and by the moon comin' up behind you, and the wind blowin' cool out o' the woods on the side o' the road; the baby fast asleep in my arms, and the other children talkin' with each other about what they'd seen, and Abram drivin' slow over the rough places, and lookin' back every once in a while to see if we was all there. It's a curious thing, honey; I liked fairs as well as anybody, and I reckon I saw all there was to be seen, and heard everything there was to be heard every time I went to one. But now, when I git to callin' 'em up, it appears to me that the best part of it all, and the part I ricollect the plainest, was jest the goin' there and the comin' back home.

"Abram knew I liked to stay till everything was over, and he'd git somebody to water and feed the stock, and then I never had any hot suppers to git while the fair lasted; so there wasn't anything to hurry me and Abram. I ricollect Maria Petty come up one day about five o'clock, jest as we was lookin' at the last race, and says she, 'I'm about to drop, Jane; but I believe I'd ruther stay here and sleep on the floor o' the amp'itheater than to go home and cook a hot supper.' And I says, 'Dou't cook a hot supper, then.' And says she, 'Why, Silas wouldn't eat a piece o' cold bread at home to save his life or mine either.'

"There's a heap o' women to be pitied, child," said Aunt Jane, dropping a handful of shelled beans into my pan with a cheerful clatter, "but, of all things, deliver me from livin' with a man that has to have hot bread three times a day. Milly Amos used to say that when she died she wanted a hot biscuit carved on her tombstone; and that if it wasn't for hot biscuits, there'd be a mighty small crop of widowers. Sam, you see, was another man that couldn't eat cold bread. But Sam had a right to his hot biscuits; for if Milly didn't feel like goin' into the kitchen, Sam'd go out and mix up his biscuits and bake 'em himself. Sam's soda biscuits was as good as mine; and when it come to beaten biscuits, why nobody could equal Sam. Milly'd make up the dough as stiff as she could handle it, and Sam'd beat it till it was soft enough to roll out; and such biscuits I never expect to eat again — white and light as snow inside, and crisp as a cracker outside. Folks nowadays makes beaten biscuits by machinery, but they don't taste like the old-fashioned kind that was beat by hand.

"And talkin' about biscuits, child, reminds me of the cookin' I used to do for the fairs. I don't reckon many women likes to remember the cookin' they've done. When folks git to rememberin', it looks like the only thing they want to call up is the pleasure they've had, the picnics and the weddin's and the tea-parties. But somehow the work I've done in my day is jest as precious to me as the play I've had. I hear young folks complainin' about havin' to work so hard, and I say to 'em, 'Child, when you git to be as old as I am, and can't work all you want to, you'll know there ain't any pleasure like good hard work.'

"There's one thing that bothers me, child," and Aunt Jane's voice sank to a confidential key: "I've had a plenty o' fears in my life, but they've all passed over me; and now there's jest one thing I'm afraid of: that I'll live to be too old to work. It appears to me like I could stand anything but that. And if the time ever comes when I can't help myself, nor other folks either, I trust the Lord'll see fit to call me hence and give me a new body, and start me to work again right away.

"But, as I was sayin', I always enjoyed cookin', and it's a pleasure to me to set and think about the hams I've b'iled and the salt-risin' bread I've baked and the old-fashioned pound-cake and sponge-cake and all the rest o' the things I used to take to the fair. Abram was always mighty proud o' my cookin', and we generally had a half a dozen or more o' the town folks to eat dinner with us every day o' the fair. Old Judge Grace and Dr. Brigham never failed to eat with us. The old judge'd say something about my salt-risin' bread every time I'd meet him in town. The first year my bread took the premium, Abram sent the premium loaf to him with the blue ribbon tied around it. After Abram died I stopped goin' to the fairs, and I don't know how many years it'd been since I set foot on the grounds. I hadn't an idea how things'd changed since my day till, year before last, Henrietta and her husband come down here from Danville. He'd come to show some blooded stock, and she come along with him to see me. And says she, 'Grandma, you've got to go to the fair with me one day, anyhow;' and I went more to please her than to please myself.

"I'm always contendin', child, that this world's growin' better and better all the time; but, Lord! Lord! that fair come pretty near upsettin' my faith. Why, in my day folks could take their children to the fair and turn 'em loose; and, if they had sense enough to keep from under the horses' feet, they was jest as safe at the fair as they was at a May meetin'. But, la! the sights I saw that day Henrietta took me to the fair! Every which way you'd look there was some sort of a trap for temptin' boys and leadin' 'em astray. Whisky and beer and all sorts o' gamblin' machines and pool sellin', and little boys no higher'n that smokin' little white cigyars, and offerin' to bet with each other on the races. And I says to Henrietta, 'Child, I don't call this a fair; why, it's jest nothin' but a gamblin' den and a whisky saloon. And,' says I, 'I know now what old Uncle Henry Matthews meant.' I'd asked the old man if he was goin' to show anything at the fair that year, and he said, 'No, Jane. Unless you've got somethin' for the town folks to bet on, it ain't worth while.'

"But there was one thing I did enjoy that day, and that was the races. There's some folks thinks that racin' horses is a terrible sin; but I don't. It's the bettin' and the swearin' that goes with the racin' that's

178

the sin. If folks'd behave as well as the horses behaves, a race'd be jest as religious as a Sunday-school picnic. There ain't a finer sight to me than a blooded horse goin' at a two-forty gait round a smooth track, and the sun a-shinin' and the flags a-wavin' and the wind blowin' and the folks cheerin' and hollerin'. So, when Henrietta said the races was goin' to begin, I says, says I, 'Here, child, take hold o' my arm and help me down these steps; I'm goin' to see one more race before I die.' And Henrietta helped me down, and we went over to the grand stand and got a good seat where I could see the horses when they come to the finish. I tell you, honey, it made me feel young again jest to see them horses coverin' the ground like they did. My father used to raise fine horses, and Abram used to say that when it come to knowin' a horse's p'ints, he'd back me against any man in Kentucky. I'll have to be a heap older'n I am now before I see the day when I wouldn't turn around and walk a good piece to look at a fine horse."

And the old lady gave a laugh at this confession of weakness.

"It was like old times to see the way them horses run. And when they come to the finish I was laughin' and hollerin' as much as anybody. And jest then somebody right behind me give a yell, and says he:

"'Hurrah for old Kentucky! When it comes to fine horses and fine whisky and fine women, she can't be beat.'

"Everybody begun to laugh, and a man right in front o' me says, 'It's that young feller from Lexin'ton. His father's one o' the biggest horsemen in the state. That's his horse that's jest won the race.' And I turned around to see, and there was a boy about the size o' my youngest grandchild up at Danville. His hat was set on the back of his head, and his hair was combed down over his eyes till he looked like he'd come out of a feeble-minded school. He had a little white cigyar in his mouth, and you could tell by his breath that he'd been drinkin'.

"Now I ain't much of a hand for meddlin' with other folks' business, but I'd been readin' about the Salvation Army, and how they preach on the street; and it come into my head that here was a time for some Salvation work. And I says to him, says I, 'Son, there's another thing that Kentucky used to be hard to beat on, and that was fine men. But,' says I, 'betwixt the fine horses and the fine women and the fine whisky, some

180

o' the men has got to be a mighty common lot.' Says I, 'Holler as much as you please for that horse out there; he's worth hollerin' for. But,' says I, 'when a state's got to raisin' a better breed o' horses than she raises men, it ain't no time to be hollerin' "hurrah" for her.' Says I, 'You're your father's son, and yonder's your father's horse; now which do you reckon your father's proudest of to-day, his horse or his son?'

"Well, folks begun to laugh again, and the boy looked like he wanted to say somethin' sassy, but he couldn't git his wits together enough to think up anything. And I says, says I, 'That horse never touched whisky or tobacco in his life; he's clean-blooded and clean-lived, and he'll live to a good old age; and, maybe, when he dies they'll bury him like a Christian, and put a monument up over him like they did over Ten Broeck. But you, why, you ain't hardly out o' your short pants, and you're fifty years old if you're a day. You'll bring your father's gray hairs in sorrow to the grave, and you'll go to your own grave a heap sooner'n you ought to, and nobody'll ever build a monument over you.'

"There was three or four boys along with the Lexin'ton boy, and one of 'em that appeared to have less whisky in him than the rest, he says, 'Well, grandma,

I reckon you're about right; we're a pretty bad lot.' And says he, 'Come on, boys, and let's git out o' this.' And off they went; and whether my preachin' ever did 'em any good I don't know, but I couldn't help sayin' what I did, and that's the last time I ever went to these new-fashioned fairs they're havin' nowadays. Fair time used to mean a heap to me, but now it don't mean anything but jest to put me in mind o' old times."

Just then there was a sound of galloping hoofs on the pike, and loud "whoas" from a rider in distress. We started up with the eagerness of those whose lives have flowed too long in the channels of stillness and peace. Here was a possibility of adventure not to be lost for any consideration. Aunt Jane dropped her pan with a sharp clang; I gathered up my skirt with its measure of unshelled beans, and together we rushed to the front of the house.

It was a "solitary horseman," wholly and ludicrously at the mercy of his steed, a mischievous young horse that had never felt the bridle and bit of a trainer.

"It's that red-headed boy of Joe Crofton's," chuckled Aunt Jane. "Nobody'd ever think he was born in Kentucky; now, would they? Old Man Bob Crawford used to say that every country boy in this state was a sort o' half-brother to a horse. But that boy yonder ain't no kin to the filly he's tryin' to ride. There's good blood in that filly as sure's you're born. I can tell by the way she throws her head and uses her feet. She'll make a fine saddle-mare, if her master ever gets hold of her. Jest look yonder, will you?"

The horse had come to a stand; she gave a sudden backward leap, raised herself on her hind legs, came down on all fours with a great clatter of hoofs, and began a circular dance over the smooth road. Round she went, stepping as daintily as a maiden at a May-day dance, while the rider clung to the reins, dug his bare heels into the glossy sides of his steed, and yelled "whoa," as if his salvation lay in that word. Then, as if just awakened to a sense of duty, the filly eeased her antics, tossed her head with a determined air, and broke into a brisk, clean gallop that would have de-lighted a skilled rider, but seemed to bring only fresh dismay to the soul of Joe Crofton's boy. His arms flapped dismally and hopelessly up and down; a gust of wind seized his ragged cap and tossed it impishly on one of the topmost boughs of the Osage-orange hedge; his protesting "whoa" voiced the hopelessness of one who resigns himself to the power of a dire fate, and he disappeared ingloriously in a cloud of summer dust. Whereupon we returned to the prosaic work of bean-shelling, with the feeling of those who have watched the curtain go down on the last scene of the comedy.

"I declare to goodness," sighed Aunt Jane breathlessly, as she stooped to recover her pan, "I ain't laughed so much in I don't know when. It reminds me o' the time Sam Amos rode in the t'u'nament." And she began laughing again at some recollection in which I had no part.

"Now, that's right curious, ain't it? When I set here talkin' about fairs, that boy comes by and makes me think o' how Sam rode at the fair that year they had the t'u'nament. I don't know how long it's been since I thought o' that ride, and maybe I never would 'a' thought of it again if that boy of Joe Crofton's hadn't put me in mind of it."

I dropped my butter-beans for a moment and assumed a listening attitude, and without any further solicitation, and in the natural course of events, the story began.

"You see the town folks was always gittin' up somethin' new for the fair, and that year I'm talkin' about it was a t'u'nament. All the Goshen folks that went

to town the last County Court day before the fair come
back with the news that there was goin' to be a t'u'nament the third day o' the fair. Everybody was sayin',
'What's that?' and nobody could answer 'em till Sam
Crawford went to town one Saturday jest before the
fair, and come back with the whole thing at his tongue's
end. Sam heard that they was practisin' for the t'u'nament that evenin', and as he passed the fair grounds on
his way home, he made a p'int of goin' in and seein'
what they was about. He said there was twelve young
men, and they was called knights; and they had a lot
o' iron rings hung from the posts of the amp'itheater,
and they'd tear around the ring like mad and try to
stick a pole through every ring and carry it off with 'em,
and the one that got the most rings got the blue ribbon.
Sam said it took a good eye and a steady arm and a
good seat to manage the thing, and he enjoyed watchin'
'em. 'But,' says he, 'why they call the thing a t'u'nament is more'n I could make out. I stayed there a
plumb hour, and I couldn't hear nor see anything that
sounded or looked like a tune.'

"Well, the third day o' the fair come, and we was all
on hand to see the t'u'nament. It went off jest like
Sam said. There was twelve knights, all dressed in

black velvet, with gold and silver spangles, and they galloped around and tried to take off the rings on their long poles. When they got through with that, the knights they rode up to the judges with a wreath o' flowers on the ends o' their poles — lances, they called 'em — and every knight called out the name o' the lady that he thought the most of; and she come up to the stand, and they put the wreath on her head, and there was twelve pretty gyirls with flowers on their heads, and they was 'Queens of Love and Beauty.' It was a mighty pretty sight, I tell you; and the band was playin' 'Old Kentucky Home,' and everybody was hollerin' and throwin' up their hats. Then the knights galloped around the ring once and went out at the big gate, and come up and promenaded around the amp'itheater with the gyirls they had crowned. The knight that got the blue ribbon took off ten rings out o' the fifteen. He rode a mighty fine horse, and Sam Amos, he says, 'I believe in my soul if I'd 'a' been on that horse I could 'a' taken off every one o' them rings.' Sam was a mighty good rider, and Milly used to say that the only thing that'd make Sam enjoy ridin' more'n he did was for somebody to put up lookin'-glasses so he could see himself all along the road.

"Well, the next thing on the program was the gentleman riders' ring. The premium was five dollars in gold for the best gentleman rider. We was waitin' for that to commence, when Uncle Jim Matthews come up, and says he, 'Sam, there's only one entry in this ring, and it's about to fall through.'

"You see they had made a rule that year that there shouldn't be any premiums given unless there was some competition. And Uncle Jim says, 'There's a young feller from Simpson County out there mighty anxious to ride. He come up here on purpose to git that premium. Suppose you ride ag'inst him and show him that Simpson can't beat Warren.' Sam laughed like he was mightily pleased, and says he, 'I don't care a rap for the premium, Uncle Jim, but, jest to oblige the man from Simpson, I'll ride. But,' says he, 'I ought to 'a' known it this mornin' so I could 'a' put on my Sunday clothes.' And Uncle Jim says, 'Never mind that; you set your horse straight and carry yourself jest so, and the judges won't look at your clothes.' 'How about the horse?' says Sam. 'Why,' says Uncle Jim, 'there's a dozen or more good-lookin' saddle-horses out yonder outside the big gate, and you can have your pick.' So Sam started off, and the next thing him and the man from Simpson was trottin' around the ring. Us Goshen people kind o' kept together when we set down in the amp'itheater. Every time Sam'd go past us, we'd all holler 'hurrah!' for him. The Simpson man appeared to have a lot o' friends on the other side o' the amp'itheater, and they'd holler for him, and the town folks was divided up about even.

"Both o' the men rode mighty well. They put their horses through all the gaits, rackin' and pacin' and lopin', and it looked like it was goin' to be a tie, when all at once the band struck up 'Dixie,' and Sam's horse broke into a gallop. Sam didn't mind that; he jest pushed his hat down on his head and took a firm seat, and seemed to enjoy it as much as anybody. But after he'd galloped around the ring two or three times, he tried to rein the horse in and get him down to a nice steady trot like the Simpson man was doin'. But, no, sir. That horse hadn't any idea of stoppin'. The harder the band played the faster he galloped; and Uncle Jim Matthews says, 'I reckon Sam's horse thinks it's another t'u'nament.' And Abram says, 'Goes like he'd been paid to gallop jest that way; don't he, Uncle Jim?'

"But horses has a heap o' sense, child; and it looked

188

to me like the horse knew he had Sam Amos, one o' the best riders in the county, on his back and he was jest playin' a little joke on him.

"Well, of course when the judges seen that Sam'd lost control of his horse, they called the Simpson man up and tied the blue ribbon on him. And he took off his hat and waved it around, and then he trotted around the ring, and the Simpson folks hollered and threw up their hats. And all that time Sam's horse was tearin' around the ring jest as hard as he could go. Sam's hat was off, and I ricollect jest how his hair looked, blowin' back in the wind — Milly hadn't trimmed it for some time — and him gittin' madder and madder every minute. Of course us Goshen folks was mad, too, because Sam didn't git the blue ribbon; but we had to laugh, and the town folks and the Simpson folks they looked like they'd split their sides. Old Man Bob Crawford jest laid back on the benches and hollered and laughed till he got right purple in the face. And says he, 'This beats the Kittle Creek babtizin' all to pieces.'

"Well, nobody knows how long that horse would 'a' kept on gallopin', for Sam couldn't stop him; but finally two o' the judges they stepped out and headed him off and took hold o' the bridle and led him out o' the ring. And Uncle Jim Matthews he jumps up, and says he, 'Let me out o' here. I want to see Sam when he gits off o' that horse.' Milly was settin' on the top seat considerably higher'n I was. And says she, 'I wouldn't care if I didn't see Sam for a week to come. Sam don't git mad often,' says she, 'but when he does, folks'd better keep out o' his way.'

"Well, Uncle Jim started off, and the rest of us set still and waited; and pretty soon here come Sam lookin' mad enough to fight all creation, sure enough. Everybody was still laughin', but nobody said anything to Sam till up comes Old Man Bob Crawford with about two yards o' blue ribbon. He'd jumped over into the ring and got it from the judges as soon as he could quit laughin'. And says he, 'Sam, I have seen gracefuler riders, and riders that had more control over their horses, but,' says he, 'I never seen one yet that stuck on a horse faithfuler'n you did in that little t'u'nament o' yours jest now; and I'm goin' to tie this ribbon on you jest as a premium for stickin' on, when you might jest as easy 'a' fell off.' Well, everybody looked for Sam to double up his fist and knock Old Man Bob down, and he might 'a' done it, but Milly saw how things was goin', and she come hurryin' up. Milly was

190

a mighty pretty woman, and always dressed herself neat and trim, but she'd been goin' around with little Sam in her arms, and her hair was fallin' down, and she looked like any woman'd look that'd carried a heavy baby all day and dragged her dress over a dusty floor. She come up, and says she, 'Well, Sam, ain't you goin' to crown me "Queen o' Love and Beauty"?' Folks used to say that Sam never was so mad that Milly couldn't make him laugh, and says he, 'You look like a queen o' love and beauty, don't you?' Of course that turned the laugh on Milly, and then Sam come around all right. And says he, 'Well, neighbors, I've made a fool o' myself, and no mistake; and you all can laugh as much as you want to;' and he took Old Man Bob's blue ribbon and tied it on little Sam's arm, and him and Milly walked off together as pleasant as you please. And that's how Sam Amos rode in the t'u'na-ment," said Aunt Jane conclusively, as she arose from her chair and shook a lapful of bean pods into a willow basket near by.

"Is Sam Amos living yet?" I asked, in the hope of prolonging an o'er-short tale. A softened look came over Aunt Jane's face.

"No, child," she said quietly, "Sam's oldest son is

livin' yet, and his three daughters. They all moved out o' the Goshen neighborhood long ago. But Sam's been in his grave twenty years or more, and here I set laughin' about that ride o' his. Somehow or other I've outlived nearly all of 'em. And now when I git to callin' up old times, no matter where I start out, I'm pretty certain to end over in the old buryin'-ground yonder. But then," and she smiled brightly, "there's a plenty more to be told over on the other side."

VIII

MARY ANDREWS' DINNER–PARTY

VIII

MARY ANDREWS' DINNER-PARTY

"WELL!" exclaimed Aunt Jane, as she surveyed her dinner-table, "looks like Mary Andrews' dinner-party, don't it? However, there's a plenty of it such as it is, and good enough what there is of it, as the old man said; so set down, child, and help yourself."

A loaf of Aunt Jane's salt-rising bread, a plate of golden butter, a pitcher of Jersey milk, and a bowl of honey in the comb, — who would ask for more? And as I sat down I blessed the friendly rain that had kept me from going home.

"But who was Mary Andrews? and what about her dinner-party?" I asked, as I buttered my bread.

"Eat your dinner, child, and then we'll talk about Mary Andrews," laughed Aunt Jane. "If I'd 'a' thought before I spoke, which I hardly ever do, I wouldn't 'a' mentioned Mary Andrews, for I know you won't let me see any rest till you know all about her."

And Aunt Jane was quite right. A summer rain, and a story, too!

"I reckon there's mighty few livin' that ricollect about Mary Andrews and her dinner-party," she said meditatively an hour later, when the dishes had been washed and we were seated in the old-fashioned parlor.

"Mary Andrews' maiden name was Crawford. A first cousin of Sam Crawford she was. Her father was Jerry Crawford, a brother of Old Man Bob, and her mother was a Simpson. People used to say that the Crawfords and the Simpsons was like two mud-puddles with a ditch between, always runnin' together. I ricollect one year three Crawford sisters married three

Simpson brothers. Mary was about my age, and she married Harvey Andrews a little over a year after me and Abram married, and there's few women I ever knew better and liked more than I did Mary Andrews.

"I ricollect her weddin' nearly as well as I do my own. My Jane was jest a month old, and I had to ask mother to come over and stay with the baby while I went to the weddin'. I hadn't thought much about what I'd wear — I'd been so taken up with the baby — and I ricollect I went to the big chest o' drawers in the spare room and jerked out my weddin' dress, and says I to mother, 'There'll be two brides at the weddin'!'

"But, bless your life, when I tried to make it meet around my waist, why, it lacked four or five inches of comin' together; and mother set and laughed fit to kill, and, says she, 'Jane, that dress was made for a young girl, and you'll never be a young girl again!' And I says, 'Well, I may never fasten this dress around my waist again, but I don't know what's to hinder me from bein' a young girl all my life.'

"I wish to goodness," she went on, "that I could ricollect what I wore to Mary Andrews' weddin'. I know I didn't wear my weddin' dress, and I know I went, but to save my life I can't call up the dress I had

197

on. It ain't like me to forgit the clothes I used to wear, but I can't call it up. However, what I wore to Mary Andrews' weddin' ain't got anything to do with Mary Andrews' dinner-party.''

Aunt Jane paused and scratched her head reflectively with a knitting needle. Evidently she was loath to go on with her story till the memory of that wedding garment should return to her.

''I was readin' the other day,'' she continued,''about somethin' they've got off yonder in Washington, some sort of bureau that tells folks what the weather'll be, and warns the ships about settin' off on a voyage when there's a storm ahead. And says I to myself, 'Do you reckon they'll ever git so smart that they can tell what sort o' weather there is ahead o' two people jest married and settin' out on the voyage that won't end till death parts 'em? and what sort o' weather they're goin' to have six months from the weddin' day?' The world's gittin' wiser every day, child, but there ain't nobody wise enough to tell what sort of a husband a man's goin' to make, nor what sort of a wife a woman's goin' to make, nor how a weddin' is goin' to turn out. I've watched folks marryin' for more'n seventy years, and I don't know much more about it than I did when I was a ten-year-old child. I've seen folks marry when it looked like certain destruction for both of 'em, and all at once they'd take a turn that'd surprise everybody, and things would come out all right with 'em. There was Wick Harris and Virginia Matthews. Wick was jest such a boy as Dick Elrod, and Virginia was another Annie Crawford. She'd never done a stitch o' sewin' nor cooked a meal o' victuals in her life, and I ricollect her mother sayin' she didn't know which she felt sorriest for, Wick or Virginia, and she wished to goodness there·was a law to keep such folks from marryin'. But, bless your life! instead o' comin' to shipwreck like Dick and Annie, they settled down as steady as any old married couple you ever saw. Wick quit his drinkin' and gamblin', and Virginia, why, there wasn't a better housekeeper in the state nor a better mother'n she got to be.

"And then I've seen 'em marry when everything looked bright ahead and everybody was certain it was a good thing for both of 'em, and it turned out that everybody was wrong. That's the way it was with Mary Andrews and Harvey. Nobody had a misgivin' about it. Mary was as happy as a lark, and Harvey looked like he couldn't wait for the weddin' day, and

everybody said they was made for each other. To be
sure, Harvey was 'most a stranger in the neighborhood,
havin' moved in about a year and a half before, and we
couldn't know him like we did the Goshen boys that'd
been born and brought up there. But nobody could
say a word against him. His family down in Tennessee,
jest beyond the state line, was as good people as ever
lived, and Harvey himself was industrious and steady,
and as fine lookin' a man as you'd see in a week's
journey. Everybody said they never saw a handsomer
couple than Harvey and Mary Andrews.

"Mary was a tall, proud-lookin' girl, always carried
herself like a queen, and hadn't a favor to ask of anybody; and Harvey was half a head taller, and jest her
opposite in color. She was dark and he was light.
They was a fine sight standin' up before the preacher
that day, and everybody was wishin' 'em good luck,
though it looked like they had enough already; both
of 'em young and healthy and happy and good-lookin',
and Harvey didn't owe a cent on his farm, and Mary's
father had furnished the house complete for her. The
weddin' come off at four o'clock in the evenin', and
we all stayed to supper, and after supper Harvey and
Mary drove over to their new home. I ricollect how

Mary looked back over her shoulder and laughed at us standin' on the steps and wavin' at her and hollerin' 'good-bye.'

"It was the fashion in that day for all the neighbors to entertain a newly married couple. Some would invite 'em to dinner, and some to supper, and then the bride and groom would have to do the same for the neighbors, and then the honeymoon'd be over, and they'd settle down and go to work like ordinary folks. We had Harvey and Mary over to dinner, and they asked us to supper. I ricollect how nice the table looked with Mary's new blue and white china and some o' the old-fashioned silver that'd been in the family for generations. And the supper matched the table, for Mary wasn't the kind that expects company to satisfy their hunger by lookin' at china and silver. She was a fine cook like her mother before her. Amos and Marthy Matthews had been invited, too, and we had a real pleasant time laughin' and jokin' like folks always do about young married people. After supper we all went out on the porch, and Mary whispered to me and Marthy to come and see her china closet and pantry. You know how proud a young housekeeper is of such things. She showed us all through the back part o' the house, and we praised everything and told her it looked like old experienced housekeepin' instead of a bride's.

"Well, when we went back to the dinin'-room on our way to the porch, if there wasn't Harvey bendin' over the table countin' the silver teaspoons! A man always looks out o' place doin' such things, and I saw Mary's face turn red to the roots of her hair. But nobody said anything, and we passed on through and left Harvey still countin'. It was a little thing, but I couldn't help thinkin' how queer it was for a man that hadn't been married two weeks to leave his company and go back to the table to count spoons, and I asked myself how I'd 'a' felt if I'd found Abram countin' spoons durin' the honeymoon.

"Did you ever take a walk, child, some cloudy night when everything's covered up by the darkness, and all at once there'll be a flash o' lightnin' showin' up everything jest for a second? Well, that's the way it is with people's lives. Near as Harvey and Mary lived to me, and friendly as we were, I couldn't tell what was happenin' between 'em. But every now and then, as the months went by, and the years, I'd see or hear somethin' that was like a flash of light in a dark place. Sometimes it was jest a look, but there's mighty little a

202

look can't tell; and as for actions, you know they speak louder than words. I ricollect one Sunday Harvey and Mary was walkin' ahead o' me and Abram. There was a rough piece o' road jest in front of the church, and I heard Harvey say: 'Don't walk there, come over on the side where it's smooth.'

"I reckon Mary thought that Harvey was thinkin' of her feet, for she stepped over to the side of the road right at once and says he, 'Don't you know them stones'll wear out your shoes quicker'n anything?' And, bless your life, if Mary didn't go right back to the middle of the road, and she took particular pains to walk on the stones as far as they went. It was a little thing, to be sure, but it showed that Harvey was thinkin' more of his wife's shoes than he was of her feet, and that ain't a little thing to a woman.

"Then, again, there was the time when me and Abram was passin' Harvey's place one evenin', and a storm was comin' up, and we stopped in to keep from gittin' wet. Mary had been to town that day, and she had on her best dress. She was a woman that looked well in anything she put on. Plain clothes couldn't make her look plain, and she set off fine clothes as much as they set her off. Me and Abram took seats on the porch, and Mary went into the hall to git another chair. I heard the back hall door open and somebody come in, and then I heard Harvey's voice. Says he, 'Go up-stairs and take off that dress.' Says he, 'What's the use of wearin' out your best clothes here at home?' But before he got the last words out, Mary was on the porch with the chair in her hand, talkin' to us about her trip to town, and lookin' as unconcerned as if she hadn't heard or seen Harvey. That night I says to Abram, says I, 'Abram, did you ever have any cause to think that Harvey Andrews was a close man?'

"Abram thought a minute, and, says he, 'Why, no; I can't say I ever did. What put such a notion into your head, Jane? Harvey looks after his own interests in a trade, but he's as liberal a giver as there is in Goshen church. Besides,' says Abram, 'who ever heard of a tall, personable man like Harvey bein' close? Stingy people's always dried up and shriveled lookin'.'

"But I'd made up my mind what the trouble was between Harvey and Mary, and nothin' that Abram said could change it. I don't reckon any man knows how women feel about stinginess and closeness in their husbands. I believe most women'd rather live with a man that'd killed somebody than one that was stingy.

And then Mary never was used to anything of that kind, for her father, old man Jerry Crawford, was one o' the freest-handed men in the county. It was 'Come in and make yourself at home' with everybody that darkened his door, and for a woman, raised like Mary was, havin' to live with a man like Harvey was about the hardest thing that could 'a' happened to her. However, she had the Crawford pride, and she carried her head high and laughed and smiled as much as ever; but there's a look that tells plain enough whether a woman's married to a man or whether she's jest tied to him and stayin' with him because she can't get free; and when Mary wasn't laughin' or smilin' I could tell by her face that she wasn't as happy as we all thought she was goin' to be the day she married Harvey."

Aunt Jane paused a moment to pick up a dropped stitch.

"It's a good thing you had your dinner, honey, before I started this yarn," she said, looking at me quizzically over her glasses, "for I'll be a long time bringin' you to the dinner-party. But I've got to tell you all this rigmarole first, so you'll understand what's comin'. If I was to tell you about the dinner-party first you'd get a wrong idea about Mary. That's how folks misjudges one another. They see people doin' things that ain't right, and they up and conclude they're bad people, when if they only knew somethin' about their lives, they'd understand how to make allowance for 'em. You've got to know a heap about people's lives, child, before you can judge 'em.

"Well, along about this time, somewhere in the '60's, I reckon it must 'a' been, there was a big excitement about politics. I can't somehow ricollect what it was all about, but they had speakin's everywhere, and the men couldn't talk about anything but politics from mornin' till night. Abram was goin' in to town every week to some meetin' or speakin'; and finally they had a big rally and a barbecue at Goshen. One of the speakers was Judge McGowan, from Tennessee, and he was a cousin of Harvey Andrews on his mother's side."

Here Aunt Jane paused again.

"I wish I could ricollect what it was all about," she said musingly. "Must 'a' been something mighty important, but it's slipped my memory, sure. I do ricollect, though, hearin' Sam Amos say to old Squire Bentham, 'What's the matter, anyhow? Ain't Kentucky politicians got enough gift o' gab, without sendin' down to Tennessee to git somebody to help you out?'

MARY ANDREWS' DINNER–PARTY

"And the old Squire laughed fit to kill; and says he, 'It's all on your account, Sam. We heard you was against us, and we knew there wasn't an orator in Kentucky that could make you change your mind. So we've sent down to Tennessee for Judge McGowan, and we're relyin' on him to bring you over to our side.' And that like to 'a' tickled Sam to death.

"Well, when Harvey heard his cousin was to be one o' the big men at the speakin', he was mighty proud, as anybody would 'a' been, and nothin' would do but he must have Judge McGowan to eat dinner at his house.

"Some of the men objected to this, and said the speakers ought to eat at the barbecue. But Harvey said that blood was thicker than water with him, and no cousin o' his could come to Goshen and go away without eatin' a meal at his house. So it was fixed up that everybody else was to eat at the barbecue, and Harvey was to take Judge McGowan over to his house to a family dinner-party.

"I dropped in to see Mary two or three days before the speakin', and when I was leavin', I said, 'Mary, if there's anything I can do to help you about your dinner-party, jest let me know.' And she said, 'There ain't a thing to do; Harvey's been to town and bought everything he could think of in the way of groceries, and Jane Ann's comin' over to cook the dinner; but thank you, all the same.'

"I thought Mary looked pleased and satisfied, and I says, 'Well, with everything to cook and Jane Ann to cook it, there won't be anything lackin' about that dinner.' And Mary laughed, and says she, 'You know I'm my father's own child.'

"Old Jerry used to say, ''Tain't no visit unless you waller a bed and empty a plate.' They used tell it that Aunt Maria, the cook, never had a chance to clean up the kitchen between meals, and the neighbors all called Jerry's house the free tavern. I've heard folks laugh many a time over the children recitin' the Ten Commandments Sunday evenin's, and Jerry would holler at 'em when they got through and say:

"'The 'leventh commandment for Kentuckians is, "Be not forgetful to entertain strangers," and never mind about 'em turnin' out to be angels. Plain folks is good enough for me.'

"Here I am strayin' off from the dinner, jest like I always do when I set out to tell anything or go anywhere. Abram used to say that if I started to the spring-house, I'd go by way o' the front porch and the front yard and the back porch and the back yard and the flower gyarden and the vegetable gyarden to git there.

"Well, the day come, and Judge McGowan made a fine speech, and Harvey carried him off in his new buggy, as proud as a peacock. I ricollect when I set down to my table that day I said to myself: 'I know Judge McGowan's havin' a dinner to-day that'll make him remember Kentucky as long as he lives.' And it wasn't till years afterwards that I heard the truth about that dinner. Jane Ann herself told me, and I don't believe she ever told anybody else. Jane Ann was crippled for a year or more before she died, and the neighbors had to do a good deal of nursin' and waitin' on her. I was makin' her a cup o' tea one day, and the kittle was bubblin' and singin', and she begun to laugh, and says she, 'Jane, do you hear that sparrer chirpin' in the peach tree there by the window?' Says she, 'I never hear a sparrer chirpin' and a kittle b'ilin', that I don't think o' the dinner Mary Andrews had the day Judge McGowan spoke at the big barbecue.' Says she, 'Mary's dead, and Harvey's dead, and I reckon there ain't any harm in speakin' of it now.' And then she told me the story I'm tellin' you.

"She said she went over that mornin' bright and early, and there was Mary sittin' on the back porch, sewin'. The house was all cleaned up, and there was a big panful o' greens on the kitchen table, but not a sign of a company dinner anywhere in sight. Jane Ann said Mary spoke up as bright and pleasant as possible, and told her to set down and rest herself, and she went on sewin', and they talked about this and that for a while, and finally Jane Ann rolled up her sleeves, and says she, 'I'm a pretty fast worker, Mis' Andrews, but a company dinner ain't any small matter; don't you think it's time to begin work?'

"And Mary jest smiled and said in her easy way, 'No, Jane Ann, there's not much to do. It won't take long for the greens to cook, and I want you to make some of your good corn bread to go with 'em.' And then she went on sewin' and talkin', and all Jane Ann could do was to set there and listen and wonder what it all meant.

"Finally the clock struck eleven, and Mary rolled up her work, and says she, 'You'd better make up your fire now, Jane Ann, and I'll set the table. Harvey likes an early dinner.'

"Jane Ann said she expected to see Mary get out the

best china and silver and the finest tablecloth and napkins she had, but instead o' that she put on jest plain, everyday things. Everything was clean and nice, but it wasn't the way to set the table for a company dinner, and nobody knew that better than Mary Andrews.

"Jane Ann said she saw a ham and plenty o' vegetables and eggs in the pantry, and she could hardly keep her hands off 'em, and she did smuggle some potatoes into the stove after she got her greens washed and her meal scalded. She said she knew somethin' was wrong, but all she could do was to hold her tongue and do her work. That was Jane Ann's way. When Mary got through settin' the table, she went up-stairs and put on her best dress. Trouble hadn't pulled her down a bit; and, if anything, she was handsomer than she was the day she married. I reckon it was her spirit that kept her from breakin' and growin' old before her time. Jane Ann said she come down-stairs, her eyes sparklin' like a girl's and a bright color in her cheeks, and she had on a flowered muslin dress, white ground with sprigs o' lilac all over it, and lace in the neck, and angel sleeves that showed off her arms, and her hair was twisted high up on her head, and a big tortoise-shell comb in it. Jane Ann said she looked as pretty as a picture; and jest as she come down the stairs, Harvey drove up with Judge McGowan, and Mary walked out to give him a welcome, while Harvey put away the buggy. Nobody had pleasanter ways than Mary Andrews. She always had somethin' to say, and it was always the right thing to be said, and in a minute her and the old judge was laughin' like they'd known each other all their lives, and he had the children on his knees trottin' 'em and tellin' 'em about his little girl and boy at home.

"Jane Ann said her greens was about done and she started to put on the corn bread, but somethin' held her back. She knew corn bread and greens wasn't a fit dinner for a stranger that had been invited there, but of course she couldn't do anything without orders, and she was standin' over the stove waitin' and wonderin', when Harvey, man-like, walked in to see how dinner was gettin' on. Jane Ann said he looked at the pot o' greens and the pan of corn bread batter, and he went into the dinin'-room and saw the table all clean, but nothin' on it beyond the ordinary, and his face looked like a thunder-cloud. And jest then Mary come in all smilin', and the prettiest color in her cheeks, and

Harvey wheeled around and says he, 'What does this mean? Where's the ham I told you to cook and all the rest o' the things I bought for this dinner?'

"Jane Ann said the way he spoke and the look in his eyes would 'a' frightened most any woman but Mary; she wasn't the kind to be frightened. Jane Ann said she stood up straight, with her head thrown back and still smilin', and her voice was as clear and sweet as if she'd been sayin' somethin' pleasant. And she looked Harvey straight in the eyes, and says she, 'It means, Harvey, that what's good enough for us is good enough for your kin.' Jane Ann said that Harvey looked at her a second as if he didn't understand, and then he give a start as if he ricollected somethin', and it looked like all the blood in his body rushed to his face, and he lifted one hand and opened his mouth like he was goin' to speak. There they stood, lookin' at each other, and Jane Ann said she never saw such a look pass between husband and wife before or since. If either of 'em had dropped dead, she said, it wouldn't 'a' seemed strange.

"Honey, I read a story once about two men that had quarreled, and one of 'em picked up a little rock and put it in his pocket, and for eight years he carried that rock, and once a year he'd turn it over. And at last, one day he met the man he hated, and he took out the rock he'd been carryin' so long, and threw it at him, and it struck him dead. Now I know as well as if Mary Andrews had told me, that Harvey had said them very same words to her years before, and she'd carried 'em in her heart, jest like the man carried the stone in his pocket, waitin' till she could throw 'em back at him and hurt him as much as he hurt her. It wasn't right nor Christian. But knowin' Mary Andrews as I did, I never had a word o' blame for her. There never was a better-hearted woman than Mary, and I always thought she must 'a' gone through a heap to make her say such a thing to Harvey.

"Jane Ann said that when she worked at a place she always tried to be blind and deaf so far as family matters was concerned, and she knew that she had no business seein' or hearin' anything that went on between Harvey and Mary, but there they stood, facin' each other, and she could hear a sparrer chirpin' outside, and the tea-kittle b'ilin' on the stove, while she stood watchin' 'em, feelin' like she was charmed by a snake. She said the look in Mary's eyes and the way she smiled made her blood run cold. And Harvey couldn't stand it. He had to give in.

"Jane Ann said his hand dropped, and he turned and walked out o' the house and down towards the barn. Mary watched him till he was out o' sight, and then she went back to the front porch, and the next minute she was laughin' and talkin' with Harvey's cousin as if nothin' had happened.

"Well, for the next half hour Jane Ann said she made her two hands do the work of four, and when she put the dinner on the table it was nothin' to be ashamed of. She sliced some ham and fried it, and made coffee and soda biscuits, and poached some eggs; and when they set down to the table, and the old judge'd said grace, he looked around, and, says he: 'How did you know, cousin, that jowl and greens was my favorite dish?' And while they was eatin' the first course, Jane Ann made up pie-crust and had a blackberry pie ready by the time they was ready to eat it. The old judge was a plain man and a hearty eater, and everything pleased him.

"When they first set down, Mary says, says she: 'You'll have to excuse Harvey, Cousin Samuel; he had some farm-work to attend to and won't be in for some little time.'

"And the old judge bows and smiles across the table,

215

and, says he, 'I hadn't missed Harvey, and ain't likely to miss him when I'm talkin' to Harvey's wife.'

"Jane Ann said she never saw a meal pass off better, and when she looked at Mary jokin' and smilin' with the judge and waitin' on the children so kind and thoughtful, she could hardly believe it was the same woman that had stood there a few minutes before with that awful smile on her face and looked her husband in the eyes till she looked him down. She said she expected Harvey to step in any minute, and she kept things hot while she was washin' up the dishes. But two o'clock come and half-past two, and still no Harvey. And pretty soon here come Mary out to the kitchen, and says she:

"'I'm goin' to drive the judge to town, Jane Ann. And when you get through cleanin' up, jest close the house, and your money's on the mantelpiece in the dinin'-room.' Then she went out in the direction of the stable, and in a few minutes come drivin' back in the buggy. Jane Ann said the horse couldn't 'a' been unharnessed at all. Her and the judge got in with the two children down in front, and they drove off to catch the four-o'clock train.

"Jane Ann said she straightened everything up in

the kitchen and dinin'-room, and shut up the house, and then she went out in the yard and walked down in the direction of the stable, and there was Harvey, standin' in the stable-yard. She said his face was turned away from her, and she was glad it was, for it scared her jest to look at his back. He was standin' as still as a statue, his arms hangin' down by his sides and both hands clenched, and it looked like he'd made up his mind to stand there till Judgment Day. Jane Ann said she wondered many a time how long he stayed there, and whether he ever did come to the house.

"I ricollect how everybody was talkin' about the speakin' that day. Abram come home from the barbecue, and, says he, 'Jane, I haven't heard such a speech as that since the days of old Humphrey Marshall;' and as for the barbecue, all it needed was Judge McGowan to set at the head o' the table. But then,' says he, 'I reckon it was natural for Harvey to want to take his cousin home with him.'

"That was about four o'clock, and it wasn't more than two hours till we heard a horse gallopin' way up the pike. I'd jest washed the supper dishes, and me and Abram was out on the back porch, and I had the baby in my arms. There was somethin' in the sound o' the horse's hoofs that told me he was carryin' bad news, and I jumped up, and says I, 'Abram, some awful thing has happened.' And he says, 'Jane, are you crazy?' I could hear the sound o' the gallopin' comin' nearer and nearer, and I rushed out to the front gate with Abram follerin' after me. We looked up the road, and there was Sam Amos gallopin' like mad on that young bay mare of his. The minute he saw us he hollered out to Abram: 'Git ready as quick as you can, and go to town! Harvey Andrews has had an apoplectic stroke, and I want you to bring the undertaker out here right away.'

"I turned around to say, 'What did I tell you?' But before I could git the words out, Abram was off to saddle and bridle old Moll. That was always Abram's way. If there was anything to be done, he did it, and the talkin' and questionin' come afterwards.

"Sam stopped at the gate and got off a minute to give his horse a breathin' spell. He said he was passin' Harvey's place about five o'clock and he heard a child screamin'. 'At first,' says he, 'I didn't pay any attention to it, I'm so used to hearin' children holler. But after I got past the house I kept hearin' the child, and somethin' told me to turn back and find out what was the matter. I went in,' said he, 'and follered the sound till I come to the stable-yard, and there was Harvey, lyin' on the ground stone dead, and Mary standin' over him lookin' like a crazy woman, and the children, pore little things, screamin' and cryin' and scared half to death.'

"'The horse and buggy was standin' there, and Mary must 'a' found the body when she come back from town.

"'I got her and the children to the house,' says he; 'and then I started out to get some person to help me move the body, and, as luck would have it,' says he, 'I met the Crawford boys comin' from town, and between us we managed to get the corpse up to the house and laid it on the big settee in the front hall. And now,' says he, 'I'm goin' after Uncle Jim Matthews; and me and him and the Crawford boys'll lay the body out when the undertaker comes. And Marthy Matthews will have to come over and stay all night.

"Says I, 'Sam, how is Mary bearin' it?'

"He shook his head, and says he, 'The worst way in the world. She hasn't shed a tear nor spoke a word, and she don't seem to notice anything, not even the children. But,' says he, 'I can't stand here talkin'. There's a heap to be done yet, and Milly's. lookin' for me now.'

"And with that he got on his horse and rode off, and I went into the house to put the children to bed. Then I set down on the porch steps to wait for Abram. The sun was down by this time, and there was a new moon in the west, and it didn't seem like there could be any sorrow and sufferin' in such a quiet, happy, peaceful-lookin' world. But there was poor Mary not a mile away, and I set and grieved over her in her trouble jest like it had been my own. I didn't know what had happened that day between Harvey and Mary. But I knew that Harvey had been struck down in the prime o' life, and that Mary had found his dead body, and that was terrible enough. From what I'd seen o' their married life I knew that Mary's loss wasn't what mine would 'a' been if Abram had dropped dead that day instead o' Harvey, but a man and woman can't live together as husband and wife and father and mother without growin' to each other; and whatever Mary hadn't lost, she had lost the father of her children, and I couldn't sleep much that night for thinkin' of her.

"The day of the funeral I went over to help Mary and get her dressed in her widow's clothes. She was actin' queer and dazed, and nothin' seemed to make much impression on her. I was fastenin' her crape collar on, and she says to me: 'I reckon you think it's strange I don't cry and take on like women do when they lose their husbands. But,' says she, 'you wouldn't blame me if you knew.'

"And then she dropped her voice down to a whisper, and says she, 'You know I married Harvey Andrews. But after I married him, I found that there wasn't any such man. I haven't got any cause to cry, for the man I married ain't dead. He never was alive, and so, of course, he can't be dead.'

"And then she began to laugh; and says she, 'I don't know which is the worst: to be sorry when you ought to be glad, or glad when you ought to be sorry.'

"And I says, 'Hush, Mary, don't talk about it. I know what you mean, but other folks might not understand.'

"Mary ain't the only one, child, that's married a man, and then found out that there *wasn't any such man*. I've looked at many a bride and groom standin' up before the preacher and makin' promises for a lifetime, and I've thought to myself, 'You pore things, you! All you know about each other is your names and your faces. You've got all the rest to find out, and nobody knows what you'll find out nor what you'll do when you find it out.'

"Folks said it was the saddest funeral they ever went to. Harvey's people all lived down in Tennessee. His father and mother had died long ago, and he hadn't any near kin except a brother and a sister; and they lived too far off to come to the funeral in time. Abram said to me after we got home: 'Well, I never thought I'd help to lay a friend and neighbor in the ground and not a tear shed over him.'

"If Mary had 'a' cried, we could 'a' cried with her. But she set at the head o' the coffin with her hands folded in her lap, and her mind seemed to be away off from the things that was happenin' around her. I don't believe she even heard the clods fallin' on the coffin; and when we started away from the grave Marthy Matthews leaned over and whispered to me: 'Jane, don't Mary remind you of somebody walkin' in her sleep?'

"Mary's mother and sister hadn't been with her in her trouble, for they happened to be down in Logan visitin' a great-uncle. So Marthy and me settled it between us that she was to stay with Mary that night and I was to come over the next mornin'. You know how much there is to be done after a funeral. Well, bright and early I went over, and Marthy met me at the gate. She was goin' out as I was comin' in. Says she, 'Go right up-stairs; Mary's lookin' for you. She's more like herself this mornin'; and I'm thankful for that.'

"The minute I stepped in the door I heard Mary's voice. She'd seen me comin' in the gate and called out to me to come up-stairs. She was in the front room, her room and Harvey's, and the closet and the bureau drawers was all open, and things scattered around every which way, and Mary was down on her knees in front of an old trunk, foldin' up Harvey's clothes and puttin' 'em away. Her hands was shakin', and there was a red spot on each of her cheeks, and she had a strange look out of her eyes.

"I says to her, 'Why, Mary, you ain't fit to be doin' that work. You ought to be in bed restin'.' And says she, 'I can't rest till I get everything straightened out. Mother and sister Sally are comin',' says she, 'and I want to get everything in order before they get here.' And I says, 'Now, Mary, you lay down on the bed and I'll put these things away. You can watch me and tell me what to do, and I'll do it; but you've got to rest.'

223

So I shook everything out and folded it up as nice as I could and laid it away in the trunk, while she watched me. And once she said, 'Don't have any wrinkles in 'em. Harvey was always mighty particular about his clothes.'

"Next to layin' the body in the ground, child, this foldin' up dead folks' clothes and puttin' 'em away is one o' the hardest things people ever has to do. It's jest like when you've finished a book and shut it up and put it away on the shelf. I knew jest how Mary felt, when she said she couldn't rest till everything was put away. The life she'd lived with Harvey was over, and she was closin' up the book and puttin' it out of sight forever. Pore child! Pore child!

"Well, when I got all o' Harvey's clothes put away, I washed out the empty drawers, lined 'em with clean paper and laid some o' little Harvey's clothes in 'em, and that seemed to please Mary. The father was gone, but there was his son to take his place. Then I shut it up tight, and Mary raised herself up out o' bed and says she, 'Take hold, Jane, I'm goin' to take this to the attic right now.' And take it we did, though the trunk was heavy and the stairs so steep and narrer we had to stop and rest on every step. We pushed the trunk way back under the eaves, and it may be standin' there yet for all I know.

"When we got down-stairs, Mary drew a long breath like she'd got a big load off her mind, and says she, 'There's one more thing I want you to help me about, and then you can go home, Jane, and I'll go to bed and rest.' She took a key out of her pocket, and says she, 'Jane, this is the key to the little cabin out in the back yard. Harvey used to keep something in there, but what it was I never knew. As long as we lived together, I never saw inside of that cabin, but I'm goin' to see it now.'

"The children started to foller us when we went out on the back porch, but Mary give 'em some playthings and told 'em to stay around in the front yard till we come back. Then we went over to the far corner of the back yard where the cabin was, under a big old sycamore tree. I ricollect how the key creaked when Mary turned it, and how hard the door was to open.

"Mary started to go in first, and then she fell back, and says she, in a whisper, 'You go in first, Jane; I'm afraid.' So I went in first and Mary follered. For a minute we couldn't see a thing. There was two windows to the cabin, but they'd been boarded up from

225

the outside, and there was jest one big crack at the top
of one of the windows that let in a long streak of light,
and you could see the dust dancin' in it. The door
opened jest enough to let us in, and we both stood there
peerin' around and tryin' to see what sort of a place
we'd got into. The first thing I made out was a heap
of old rusty iron. I started to take a step, and my foot
struck against it. There was old bolts and screws and
horseshoes and scraps of old cast iron and nails of every
size, all laid together in a big heap. The place seemed
to be full of somethin', but I couldn't see what it all was
till my eyes got used to the darkness. There was a
row of nails goin' all round the wall, and old clothes
hangin' on every one of 'em. And down on the floor
there was piles of old clothes, folded smooth and laid
one on top o' the other jest like a washerwoman would
fold 'em and pile 'em up. Harvey's old clothes and
Mary's and the children's, things that any right-minded
person would 'a' put in the rag-bag or given away to
anybody that could make use of 'em; there they was,
all hoarded up in that old room jest like they was of
some value. And over in one corner was all the old
worn-out tin things that you could think of: buckets
and pans and milk-strainers and dippers and cups.

226

And next to them was all the glass and china that'd been broken in the years Mary and Harvey'd been keepin' house. And there was a lot of old brooms, nothin' but stubs, tied together jest like new brooms in the store. And there was all the children's broken toys, dolls, and doll dresses, and even some glass marbles that little Harvey used to play with. The dust was lyin' thick and heavy over everything, and the spider-webs looked like black strings hangin' from the ceilin'; but things of the same sort was all lyin' together jest like some woman had put the place in order.

"You've heard tell of that bird, child, that gathers up all sorts o' rubbish and carries it off to its nest and hides it? Well, I thought about that bird; and the heap of old iron reminded me of a little boy's pocket when you turn it wrong side out at night, and the china and glass and doll-rags made me think of the playhouses I used to make under the trees when I was a little girl. I've seen many curious places, honey, but nothin' like that old cabin. The moldy smell reminded me of the grave; and when I looked at all the dusty, old plunder, the ragged clothes hangin' against the wall like so many ghosts, and then thought of the dead man that had put 'em there, I tell you it made my flesh creep.

"Well, we stood there, me and Mary, strainin' our eyes tryin' to see into the dark corners, and all at once the meanin' of it come over me like a flash: *Harvey was a miser!*"

Aunt Jane stopped, took off her glasses and polished them on the hem of her gingham apron. I sat holding my breath; but, all regardless of my suspense, she dropped the thread of the story and followed memory in one of her capricious backward flights.

"I ricollect a sermon I heard when I was a gyirl," she said. "It ain't often, I reckon, that a sermon makes much impression on a gyirl's mind. But this wasn't any ordinary sermon or any ordinary preacher. Presbytery met in town that year, and all the big preachers in the state was there. Some of 'em come out and preached to the country churches, and old Dr. Samuel Chalmers Morse preached at Goshen. He was one o' the biggest men in the Presbytery, and I ricollect his looks as plain as I ricollect his sermon. Some preachers look jest like other men, and you can tell the minute you set eyes on 'em that they ain't any wiser or any better than common folks. But Dr. Morse wasn't that kind.

"You know the Bible tells about people walkin' with

God and talkin' with God. It says Enoch walked with God and Adam talked with Him. Some folks might find that hard to believe, but it seems jest as natural to me. Why many a time I've been in my gyarden when the sun's gone down, and it ain't quite time for the moon to come up, and the dew's fallin' and the flowers smellin' sweet, and I've set down in the summer-house and looked up at the stars; and if I'd heard a voice from heaven it wouldn't 'a' been a bit stranger to me than the blowin' of the wind.

"The minute I saw Dr. Morse I thought about Adam and Enoch, and I said to myself, 'He looks like a man that's walked with God and talked with God.'

"I didn't look at the people's hats and bonnets that day half as much as I usually did, and part of that sermon stayed by me all my life. He preached about Nebuchadnezzar and the image he saw in his dream with the head of gold and the feet of clay. And he said that every human being was like that image; there was gold and there was clay in every one of us. Part of us was human and part was divine. Part of us was earthly like the clay, and part heavenly like the gold.

229

And he said that in some folks you couldn't see anything but the clay, but that the gold was there, and if you looked long enough you'd find it. And some folks, he said, looked like they was all gold, but somewhere or other there was the clay, too, and nobody was so good but what he had his secret sins and open faults. And he said sin was jest another name for ignorance, and that Christ knew this when he prayed on the cross, 'Father, forgive them, for they know not what they do.' He said everybody would do right, if they knew what was right to do, and that the thing for us to do was to look for the gold and not the clay in other folks. For the gold was the part that would never die, and the clay was jest the mortal part that we dropped when this mortal shall have put on immortality.

"Child, that sermon's come home to me many a time when I've caught myself weighin' people in the balance and findin' 'em wantin'. That's what I'd been doin' all them years with pore Harvey. I'd seen things every once in a while that let in a little light on his life and Mary's, but the old cabin made it all plain as day, and it seemed like every piece o' rubbish in it rose up in judgment against me. I never felt like cryin' at Harvey's funeral, but when I stood there peerin' around, the tears burnt my eyes, and I says to myself, 'Clay and gold! Clay and gold!'

"The same thought must 'a' struck Mary at the same minute it did me, for she fell on her knees moanin' and wringin' her hands and cryin':

"'God forgive me! God forgive me! I see it all now. He couldn't help it, and I've been a hard woman, and God'll judge me as I judged Harvey.'

"The look in her eyes and the sound of her voice skeered me, and I saw that the quicker I got her out o' the old cabin the better. I put my hand on her shoulder, and says I, 'Hush, Mary. Get up and come back to the house; but don't let the children hear you takin' on so. You might skeer little Harvey.'

"She stopped a minute and stared at me, and then she caught hold o' my hand, and says she: 'No! no! the children mustn't ever know anything about it, and nobody must ever see the inside o' that awful place. Come, quick!' says she; and she got up from her knees and pulled me outside of the door and locked it and dropped the key in her apron pocket.

"Little Harvey come runnin' up to her, and I was in hopes the sight of the child would bring her to herself, but she walked on as if she hadn't seen him; and as

231

soon as she got up-stairs she fell down in a heap on the floor and went to wringin' her hands and beatin' her breast and cryin' without tears.

"Honey, if you're done a wrong to a livin' person, you needn't set down and grieve over it. You can go right to the person and make it right or try to make it right. But when the one you've wronged is dead, and the grave lies between you, that's the sort o' grief that breaks hearts and makes people lose their minds. And that was what Mary Andrews had to bear when she opened the door o' that old cabin and saw into Harvey's nature, and felt that she had misjudged and condemned him.

"I couldn't do anything for a long time, but jest sit by her and listen while she called Harvey back from the dead, and called on God to forgive her, and blamed herself for all that had ever gone wrong between 'em. But at last she wore herself out and had to stop, and says I, 'Mary, I don't know what's passed between you and Harvey —' And she broke in, and says she:

"'No! no! you don't know, and nobody on this earth knows what I've been through. I used to feel like I was in an iron cage that got smaller and smaller every day, and I knew the day was comin' when it would shut

in on me and crush me. But I wouldn't give in to
Harvey, I wouldn't let him have his own way, and I
fought him and hated him and despised him; and now
I see he couldn't help it, and I feel like I'd been strikin'
a crippled child.'

"A crippled child! That was jest what pore Harvey
was; but I knew it wasn't right for Mary to take all the
blame on herself, and says I:

"'Mary, if Harvey could keep other people from
knowin' what he was, couldn't he have kept you from
knowin' it, too? If he was free-handed to other
people, what was to hinder him from bein' the same
way to you?' Says I, 'If there's any blame in this
matter it belongs as much to Harvey as it does to you.
When you look at that old cabin,' says I, 'you can't
have any hard feelin's toward pore Harvey. You've
forgiven him, and now,' says I, 'there's jest one more
person you've got to forgive, and that's yourself,' says I.
'It's jest as wrong to be too hard on yourself as it is to
be too hard on other folks.'

"I never had thought o' that before, child, but I've
thought of it many a time since and I know it's true.
It ain't often you find a human bein' that's too hard on
himself. Most of us is jest the other way. But Mary

was one of that kind. I could see a change come over her face while I was talkin', and I've always believed them words was put in my mouth to give Mary the comfort and help she needed.

"She grabbed hold o' my hand, and says she:

"'Do you reckon I've got a right to forgive myself?' Says she, 'I know I'm not a mean woman by nature, but Harvey's ways wasn't my ways. He made me do things I didn't want to do and say things I didn't want to say, and I never was myself as long as I lived with him. But God knows I wouldn't 'a' been so hard on him if I'd only known,' says she. 'God may forgive me, but even if He does, it don't seem to me that I've got a right to forgive myself.'

"And says I, 'Mary, if you don't forgive yourself you won't be able to keer for the children, and you haven't got any right to wrong the livin' by worryin' over the dead. And now,' says I, 'you lie down on this bed and shut your eyes and say to yourself, "Harvey's forgiven me, and God's forgiven me, and I forgive myself." Don't let another thought come into your head. Jest say it over and over till you go to sleep, and while you're sleepin', I'll look after the children.'

"I didn't have much faith in my own remedy, but

she minded me like a child mindin' its mother; and, sure enough, when I tiptoed up-stairs an hour or so after that, I found her fast asleep. Her mother and her sister Sally come while she was still sleepin', and I left for home, feelin' that she was in good hands.

"That night about half-past nine o'clock I went outdoors and set down on the porch steps in the dark, as I always do jest before bedtime. That's been one o' my ways ever since I was a child. Abram used to say he had known me to forgit my prayers many a night, but he never knew me to forgit to go outdoors and look up at the sky. If there was a moon, or if the stars was shinin', I'd stay out and wander around in the gyarden till he'd come out after me; and if it was cloudy, I'd set there and feel safe in the darkness as in the light. I always have thought, honey, that we lose a heap by sleepin' all night. Well, I was sittin' there lookin' up at the stars, and all at once I saw a bright light over in the direction of Harvey Andrews' place. Our house was built on risin' ground, and we could see for a good ways around the country. I called Abram and asked him if he hadn't better saddle old Moll and ride over and see if he couldn't help whoever was in trouble. But he said it was most likely some o' the neighbors burnin' brush, and whatever it was it would be out before he could git to it. So we set there watchin' it and speculatin' about it till it died down, and then we went to bed.

"The next mornin' I was out in the yard weedin' out a bed o' clove pinks, and Sam Amos come ridin' by on his big bay mare. I hollered to him and asked him if he knew where the fire was the night before. And says he, 'Yes, Aunt Jane; it was that old cabin on Harvey Andrews' place.' He said that Amos Matthews happened to be goin' by at the time and took down the fence-rails to keep it from spreadin', but that was all he could do. Sam said Amos told him there was somethin' mysterious about that fire. He said it must 'a' been started from the inside, for the flames didn't burst through the windows and roof till after he got there, and the whole inside was ablaze. But, when he tried to open the door, it was locked fast and tight. He said Mary and her mother and sister was all out in the yard, and Mary was standin' with her hands folded in front of her, lookin' at the burnin' house jest as calm as if it was her own fireplace. Amos asked her for the key to the cabin door, and she went to the back porch and took one off a nail, but it wouldn't fit the lock, and

before she could get another to try, the roof was on fire
and cavin' in. Amos told Sam the cabin appeared
to be full of old plunder of all sorts, and you could smell
burnt rags for a mile around.

"Of course there was a good deal o' talk about the
fire, and everybody said how curious it was that it
could catch on the inside when the door was locked.
I never said a word, not even to Abram, but I knew well
enough who set the old cabin afire, and why the key
Mary gave Amos wouldn't fit the lock. Harvey's
clothes was packed away under the old garret; the old
cabin was burned, and the ashes and rubbish hauled
away, and there wasn't anything much left to remind
Mary of the things she was tryin' to forget. That's
the best way to do. When a thing's done and you
can't undo it, there's no use in frettin' and worryin'
yourself. Jest put it out o' your mind, and go on your
way and git ready for the next trial that's comin'
to you.

"But Mary never seemed like herself after Harvey
died, until little Harvey was taken with fever. That
seemed to rouse her and bring her senses back, and she
nursed him night and day. The little thing went down
to the very gates of death, and everybody give up hope

except the old doctor. He'd fight death off as long as there was breath in the body. The night the turnin' point was to come I set up with Mary. The child'd been moanin' and tossin', and his muscles was twitchin', and the fever jest as high as it could be. But about three o'clock he got quiet and about half-past three I leaned over and counted his breaths. He was breathin' slow and regular, and I touched his forehead and found it was wet, and the fever was goin' away. I went over to Mary, and says I, 'You go in the other room and lie down, Mary, the fever's broke, and Harvey's goin' to git well.' She stared at me like she couldn't take in what I was sayin'. Then her face begun to work like a person's in a convulsion, and she jumped up and rushed out o' the room, and the next minute she give a cry that I can hear yet. Then she begun to sob, and I knew she was cryin' tears at last, and I set by the child and cried with her.

"She wasn't able to be up for two or three days, and every little while she'd burst out cryin'. Some folks said she was cryin' for joy about the child gittin' well; and some said she was cryin' the tears she ought to 'a' cried when Harvey was buried; but I knew she was cryin' over all the sorrows of her married life. She told me afterwards that she hadn't shed a tear for six or seven years. Says she, 'I used to cry my eyes out nearly over the way things went, and one day somethin' happened and I come near cryin'; but the children was around and I didn't want them to see me; so I says to myself, "I won't cry. What's the use wastin' tears over such things?" And from that day,' says she, 'I got as hard as a stone, and it looks like I was jest turnin' back to flesh and blood again.'

"There's only two ways o' takin' trouble, child; you can laugh over it or you can cry over it. But you've got to do one or the other. The Lord made some folks that can laugh away their troubles, and he made tears for them that can't laugh, and human bein's can't harden themselves into stone.

"I reckon, as Mary said, nobody on earth knew what she'd been through, livin' with a man like Harvey. If he'd been an out-and-out miser, it would 'a' been better for everybody concerned. But it looked like Nature started out to make him a miser and then sp'iled the job, so's he was neither one thing nor the other. The gold was there, and he showed that to outsiders; and the clay was there, and he showed that to Mary. And that's the strangest part of all to me. If he had enough sense not to want his neighbors to know his meanness. it looks like he ought to have had sense enough to hide it from his wife. A man ought to want his wife to think well of him whether anybody else does or not. You see, a woman can make out to live with a man and not love him, but she can't live with him and despise him. She's jest got to respect him. But there's some men that never have found that out. They think that because a woman stands up before a preacher and promises to love and honor him, that she's bound to do it, no matter what he does. And some women do. They're like dogs; they'll stick to a man no matter what he does. Some women never can see any faults in their husbands, and some sees the faults and covers 'em up and hides 'em from outsiders. But Mary wasn't that sort. She couldn't deceive herself, and nobody could deceive her; and when she found out Harvey's meanness she couldn't help despisin' him in her heart, jest like Michal despised David when she saw him playin' and dancin' before the Lord.

"There's something I never have understood, and one of 'em is why such a woman as Mary should 'a' been permitted to marry a man like Harvey Andrews. It kind o' shakes my faith in Providence every time I think of it. But I reckon there was a reason for it, whether I can see it or not."

Aunt Jane's voice ceased. She dropped her knitting in her lap and leaned back in the old easy-chair. Apparently she was looking at the dripping syringa bush near the window, but the look in her eyes told me that she had reached a page in the story that was not for my eyes or my ears, and I held inviolate the silence that had fallen between us.

A low, far-off roll of thunder, the last note of the storm-music, roused her from her reverie.

"Sakes alive, child!" she exclaimed, starting bolt upright. "Have I been sleepin' and dreamin' and you settin' here? Well, I got through with my story, anyhow, before I dropped off."

"Surely that isn't all," I said, discontentedly. "What became of Mary Andrews after Harvey died?"

Aunt Jane laughed blithely.

"No, it ain't all. What's gittin' into me to leave off the endin' of a story? Mary was married young; and when Harvey died she had the best part of her life before her, and it was the best part, sure enough. About a year after she was left a widow she went up to Christian County to visit some of her cousins, and there she met the man she ought to 'a' married in the first place. I ain't any hand for second marriages. 'One man for one woman,' says I; but I've seen so many second marriages that was happier than any first ones that I never say anything against marryin' twice. Some folks are made for each other, but they make mistakes in the road and git lost, and don't git found till they've been through a heap o' tribulation, and, maybe, the biggest half o' their life's gone. But then, they've got all eternity before 'em, and there's time enough there to find all they've lost and more besides. But Mary found her portion o' happiness before it was too late. Elbert Madison was the man she married. He was an old bachelor, and a mighty well-to-do man, and they said every old maid and widow in Christian County had set her cap for him one time or another. But whenever folks said anything to him about marryin', he'd say, 'I'm waitin' for the Right Woman. She's somewhere in the world, and as soon as I find her I'm goin' to marry.'

"It got to be a standin' joke with the neighbors and the family, and his brother used to say that Elbert believed in that 'Right Woman' the same as he believed in God.

"'They used to tell how one Christmas, Elbert's nieces had a lot o' young company from Louisville, and they had a big dance Christmas Eve. Elbert was there, and the minute he come into the room the oldest niece, she whispered, 'Here's Uncle Elbert; he's come to see if the Right Woman's at the ball.' And with that all them gyirls rushed up to Elbert and shook hands with him and pulled him into the middle o' the room under a big bunch o' mistletoe, and the prettiest and sassiest one of 'em, she took her dress between the tips of her fingers and spread it out and made a low bow, and says she, lookin' up into Elbert's face, says she:

"'Mr. Madison, don't I look like the Right Woman?'

"Everybody laughed and expected to see Elbert blush and act like he wanted to go through the floor. But instead o' that he looked at her serious and earnest, and at last he says: 'You do look a little like her, but you ain't her. You've got the color of her eyes,' says he, 'but not the look of 'em. Her hair's dark like yours, but it don't curl quite as much, and she's taller than you are, but not quite so slim.'

"They said the gyirls stopped laughin' and jest looked at each other, and one of 'em said:

"'Well, did you ever?' And that was the last time

243

they tried to tease Elbert. But Elbert's brother he turns to somebody standin' near him, and says he, 'Unless Elbert gets that "right-woman" foolishness out of his head and marries and settles down like other men, I believe he'll end his days in a lunatic asylum.'

"But it all turned out the way Elbert said it would. The minute he saw Mary Andrews, he whispered to his sister-in-law, and says he, 'Sister Mary, do you see that dark-eyed woman over there by the door? Well, that's the woman I've been lookin' for all my life.'

"He walked across the room and got introduced to her, and they said when him and Mary shook hands they looked each other in the eyes and laughed like two old friends that hadn't met for years.

"Harvey hadn't been dead much over a year and Mary wanted to put off the weddin'. But Elbert said, 'No; I've waited for you a lifetime and I'm not goin' to wait any longer.' So they got married as soon as Mary could have her weddin' clothes made, and a happier couple you never saw. Elbert used to look at her and say:

"'God made Eve for Adam, and he made you for me.'

"And he didn't only love Mary, but he loved her

children the same as if they'd been his own. A woman that's been another man's wife can easy enough find a man to love her, but to find one that'll love the other man's children, that's a different matter."

One! two! three! four! chimed the old clock; and at the same moment out came the sun, sending long rays across the room. The rain had subsided to a gentle mist, and the clouds were rolling away before a south-west wind that carried with it fragrance from wet flowers and leaves and a world cleansed and renewed by a summer storm. We moved our chairs out on the porch to enjoy the clearing-off. There were health and strength in every breath of the cool, moist air, and for every sense but one a pleasure — odor, light, coolness, and the faint music of falling water from the roof and from the trees that sent down miniature showers when-ever the wind stirred their branches.

Aunt Jane drew a deep breath of satisfaction, and looked upward at the blue sky.

"I don't mind how much it rains durin' the day," she said, "if it'll jest stop off before night and let the sun set clear. And that's the way with life, child. If everything ends right, we can forget all about the troubles we've had before. I reckon if Mary Andrews

could 'a' seen a few years ahead while she was havin'
her trials with pore Harvey, she would 'a' borne 'em
all with a better grace. But lookin' ahead is somethin'
we ain't permitted to do. We've jest got to stand up
under the present and trust for the time we can't see.
And whether we trust or not, child, no matter how dark
it is nor how long it stays dark, the sun's goin' to come
out some time, and it's all goin' to be right at the last.
You know what the Scripture says, 'At evening time
it shall be light!'"

Her faded eyes were turned reverently toward the
glory of the western sky, but the light on her face was
not all of the setting sun.

"At evening time it shall be light!"

Not of the day but of human life were these words
spoken, and with Aunt Jane the prophecy had been
fulfilled.

IX

THE GARDENS OF MEMORY

IX

THE GARDENS OF MEMORY

EACH of us has his own way of classifying humanity. To me, as a child, men and women fell naturally into two great divisions: those who had gardens and those who had only houses.

Brick walls and pavements hemmed me in and robbed me of one of my birthrights; and to the fancy of childhood a garden was a paradise, and the people who had gardens were happy Adams and Eves walking in a golden mist of sunshine and showers, with green leaves and blue sky overhead, and blossoms springing at their

249

feet; while those others, dispossessed of life's springs, summers, and autumns, appeared darkly entombed in shops and parlors where the year might as well have been a perpetual winter.

As I grew older I learned that there was a small sub-class composed of people who not only possessed gardens, but whose gardens possessed them, and it is the spots sown and tended by these that blossom eternally in one's remembrance as veritable vailimas— "gardens of dreams."

In every one's mind there is a lonely space, almost abandoned of consciousness, the time between infancy and childhood. It is like that period when the earth was "without form, and void; and darkness was upon the face of the deep." Here, like lost stars floating in the firmament of mind, will be found two or three faint memories, remote and disconnected. With me one of these memories is of a garden. I was riding with my father along a pleasant country road. There were sunshine and a gentle wind, and white clouds in a blue sky. We stopped at a gate. My father opened it, and I walked up a grassy path to the ruins of a house. The chimney was still standing, but all the rest was a heap of blackened, half-burned rubbish which spring and summer were covering with wild vines and weeds, and around the ruins of the house lay the ruins of the garden. The honeysuckle, bereft of its trellis, wandered helplessly over the ground, and amid a rank growth of weeds sprang a host of yellow snapdragons. I remember the feeling of rapture that was mine at the thought that I had found a garden where flowers could be gathered without asking permission of any one. And as long as I live, the sight of a yellow snapdragon on a sunny day will bring back my father from his grave and make me a little child again gathering flowers in that deserted garden, which is seemingly in another world than this.

A later memory than this is of a place that was scarcely more than a paved court lying between high brick walls. But because we children wanted a garden so much, we called it by that name; and here and there a little of Mother Earth's bosom, left uncovered, gave us some warrant for the misnomer. Yet the spot was not without its beauties, and a less exacting child might have found content within its boundaries.

Here was the Indian peach tree, whose pink blossoms told us that spring had come. Its fruit in the late summer was like the pomegranate in its rich color, "blood-tinctured with a veined humanity;" and its friendly limbs held a swing in which we cleft the air like the birds. Yet even now the sight of an Indian peach brings melancholy thoughts. A yellow honeysuckle clambered over a wall. But this flower has no perfume, and a honeysuckle without perfume is a base pretender, to be cast out of the family of the real sweet-scented honeysuckle. There were two roses of similar quality, one that detestable mockery known as the burr-rose. I have for this flower the feeling of repulsion that one has for certain disagreeable human beings,— people with cold, clammy hands, for instance. I hated its feeble pink color, its rough calyx, and its odor always made me think of vast fields of snow, and icicles hanging from snow-covered roofs under leaden wintry skies. Unhappy mistake to call such a thing a rose, and plant it in a child's garden! The only place where it might fitly grow is by the side of the road that led Childe Roland to the Dark Tower: between the bit of "stubbed ground" and the marsh near to the "palsied oak," with its roots set in the "bog, clay and rubble, sand and stark black dearth."

The other rose I recall with the same dislike, though it was pleasing to the eye. The bush was tall, and had the nature of a climber; for it drooped in a lackadaisical way, and had to be tied to a stout post. I think it could have stood upright, had it chosen to do so; and its drooping seemed only an ugly habit, without grace. The cream-white flowers grew in clusters, and the buds were really beautiful, but color and form are only the body of the rose; the soul, the real self, is the rose odor, and no rose-soul was incarnated in its petals. Again and again, deceived by its beauty, I would hold it close to my face to breathe its fragrance, and always its faint sickening-sweet odor brought me only disappointment and disgust. It was a Lamia among roses. Another peculiarity was that it had very few thorns, and those few were small and weak. Yet the thorn is as much a part of the true rose as its sweetness; and lacking the rose thorn and the rose perfume, what claim had it to the rose name? I never saw this false rose elsewhere than in the false garden, and because it grew there, and because it dishonored its royal family, I would not willingly meet it face to face again.

We children cultivated sweet-scented geraniums in pots, but a flower in a pot was to me like a bird in a cage, and the fragrant geraniums gave me no more pleasure than did the scentless many-hued lady's-slippers that we planted in tiny borders, and the purple flowering beans and white blossoms of the madeira vines that grew on a tall trellis by the cistern's grassy mound. There was nothing here to satisfy my longing, and I turned hungrily to other gardens whose gates were open to me in those early days. In one of these was a vast bed of purple heartsease, flower of the beautiful name. Year after year they had blossomed and gone to seed till the harvest of flowers in their season was past gathering, and any child in the neighborhood was at liberty to pluck them by handfuls, while the wicked ones played at "chicken fighting" and littered the ground with decapitated bodies. There is no heartsease nowadays, only the magnificent pansy of which it was the modest forerunner. But one little cluster of dark, spicy blooms like those I used to gather in that old garden would be more to me than the most splendid pansy created by the florist's art.

The lily of the valley calls to mind a garden, almost in the heart of town, where this flower went forth to possess the land and spread itself in so reckless a growth that at intervals it had to be uprooted to protect the landed rights of the rest of the community. Never were there such beds of lilies! And when they pierced the black loam with their long sheath-like leaves, and broke their alabaster boxes of perfume on the feet of spring, the most careless passer-by was forced to stay his steps for one ecstatic moment to look and to breathe, to forget and to remember. The shadow of the owner's house lay on this garden at the morning hour, and a tall brick building intercepted its share of the afternoon sunshine; but the love and care of the wrinkled old woman who tended it took the place of real sunshine, and everything planted here grew with a luxuriance not seen in sunnier and more favored spots. The mistress of the garden, when questioned as to this, would say it was because she gave her flowers to all who asked, and the God of gardens loved the cheerful giver and blessed her with an abundance of bud and blossom. The highest philosophy of human life she used in her management of this little plant world; for, burying the weeds at the roots of the flowers, the evil was made to minister to the good; and the nettle, the plantain and all their kind were transmuted by nature's fine chemistry into pinks, lilies, and roses.

The purple splendor of the wistaria recalls the garden that I always entered with a fearful joy, for here a French gardener reigned absolute, and the flowers might be looked at, but not pulled. How different from those wild gardens of the neighboring woods where we children roamed at will, shouting rapturously over the finding of a bed of scentless blue violets or delicate anemones that withered and were thrown away before we reached home,— an allegory, alas! of our later lives.

There was one garden that I coveted in those days as Ahab coveted his neighbor's vineyard. After many years, so many that my childish longing was almost forgotten, I had it, I and my children. Together we played under the bee-haunted lindens, and looked at the sunset through the scarlet and yellow leaves of the sugar maples, and I learned that "every desire is the prophecy of its own fulfilment;" and if the fulfilment is long delayed, it is only that it may be richer and deeper when it does come.

All these were gardens of the South; but before childhood was over I watched the quick, luxuriant growth of flowers through the brief summer of a northern clime. The Canterbury-bell, so like a prim, pretty maiden, the dahlia, that stately dame always in court costume of gorgeous velvet, remind me of those well-kept beds where not a leaf or flower was allowed to grow awry; and in one ancient garden the imagination of a child found wings for many an airy flight. The town itself bore the name of the English nobleman, well known in Revolutionary days. Not far away his, mansion sturdily defied the touch of time and decay, and admonished the men of a degenerate present to remember their glorious past. The house that sheltered me that summer was known in colonial days as the Black-Horse Tavern. Its walls had echoed to the tread of patriot and tory, who gathered here to drink a health to General Washington or to King George; and patriot, and tory, too, had trod the paths of the garden and plucked its flowers and its fruit in the times that tried men's souls. By the back gate grew a strawberry apple tree, and every morning the dewy grass held a night's windfall of the tiny red apples that were the reward of the child who rose earliest. A wonderful grafted tree that bore two kinds of fruit gave the place a touch of fairyland's magic, and no explanation of the process of grafting ever diminished the awe I felt when I stood under this tree and saw ripe spice apples growing on one limb and green winter pearmains on all the others. The pound sweeting. the spitzenberg, and many sister apples were there; and I stayed long enough to see them ripen into perfection. While they ripened I gathered the jewel-like clusters of red and white currants and a certain rare English gooseberry which English hands had brought from beyond the seas and planted here when the sign of the Black-Horse swung over the tavern door. The ordinary gooseberry is a plebeian fruit, but this one was more patrician than its name, and its name was "the King George." Twice as large as the common kind, translucent and yellowish white when fully ripe, and of an incomparable sweetness and flavor, it could have graced a king's table and held its own with the delicate strawberry or the regal grape. And then, best of all, it was a forbidden fruit, whereof we children ate by stealth, and solemnly declared that we had not eaten. Could the Garden of the Hesperides have held more charms?

At the end of the long Dutch "stoop" I found the wands of he snowberry, whose tiny flowers have the odor and color of the trailing arbutus, and whose waxen berries reminded me of the crimson "buckberry" of Southern fields. Fuchsias and dark-red clove pinks grew in a peculiarly rich and sunny spot by the back fence, and over a pot of the muskplant I used to hang as Isabella hung over her pot of basil. I had never seen it before, and have never seen it since, but by the witchery of perfume one of its yellow flowers, one of its soft pale green leaves could place me again in that garden of the old inn, a child walking among the ghosts and memories of a past century.

In all these flowery closes there are rich aftermaths; but when Memory goes a-gleaning, she dwells longest on the evenings and mornings once spent in Aunt Jane's garden.

"I don't reckon Solomon was thinkin' about flower gyardens when he said there was a time for all things," Aunt Jane was wont to say, "but anyhow it's so. You know the Bible says that the Lord God walked in the gyarden of Eden in 'the cool of the day,' and that's the best time for seein' flowers,— the cool of the mornin' and the cool of the evenin'. There's jest as much difference between a flower with the dew on it at sun-up and a flower in the middle o' the day as there is between a woman when she's fresh from a good night's sleep and when she's cookin' a twelve-o'clock dinner in a hot kitchen. You think them poppies are mighty pretty with the sun shinin' on 'em, but the poppy ain't a sun flower; it's a sunrise flower."

And so I found them when I saw them in the faint light of a summer dawn, delicate and tremulous, like lovely apparitions of the night that an hour of sun will dispel. With other flowers the miracle of blossoming is performed so slowly that we have not time to watch its every stage. There is no precise moment when the rose leaves become a bud, or when the bud turns to a full-blown flower. But at dawn by a bed of poppies you may watch the birth of a flower as it slips from the calyx, casting it to the ground as a soul casts aside its outgrown body, and smoothing the wrinkles from its silken petals, it faces the day in serene beauty, though the night of death be but a few hours away.

"And some evenin' when the moon's full and there's a dew fallin'," continued Aunt Jane, "that's the time to see roses, and to smell roses, too. And chrysanthemums, they're sun-down flowers. You come into my gyarden about the first o' next November, child, some evenin' when the sun's goin' down, and you'll see the white ones lookin' like stars, and the yeller ones shinin' like big gold lamps in the dusk; and when the last light o' the sun strikes the red ones, they look like cups o' wine, and some of 'em turn to colors that there ain't any names for. Chrysanthemums jest match the red and yel'er leaves on the trees, and the colors you see in the sky after the first frosts when the cold weather begins to set in. Yes, honey, there's a time and a season for everything; flowers, too, jest as Solomon said."

An old garden is like an old life. Who plants from youth to age writes a record of the years in leaf and blossom, and the spot becomes as sacred as old wine, old books, and old friends Here in the garden of Aunt Jane's planting I found that flowers were also memories; that reminiscences were folded in the petals of roses and lilies; that a rose's perfume might be a voice from a vanished summer; and even the snake gliding across our path might prove a messenger bearing a story of other days. Aunt Jane made a pass at it with her hoe, and laughed as the little creature disappeared on the other side of the fence.

"I never see a striped snake," she said, "that I don't think o' Sam Amos and the time he saw snakes. It wasn't often we got a joke on Sam, but his t'u'nament and his snake kept us laughin' for many a day.

"Sam was one o' them big, blunderin' men, always givin' Milly trouble, and havin' trouble himself, jest through pure keerlessness. He meant well; and Milly used to say that if what Sam did was even half as good as what Sam intended to do, there'd be one perfect man on God's earth One of his keerless ways was scatterin' his clothes all over the house. Milly'd scold and fuss about it, but Sam got worse instead o' better up to the day he saw the snake, and after that Milly said there wasn't a more orderly man in the state. The way of it was this: Sam was raisin' an embankment 'round one of his ponds, and Uncle Jim Matthews and Amos Crawford was helpin' him. It was one Monday mornin', about the first of April, and the weather was warm and sunny, jest the kind to bring out snakes. I reckon there never was anybody hated a snake as much as Sam did. He'd been skeered by one when he was a child, and never got over it. He used to say there was jest two things he was afraid of: Milly and a snake. That mornin' Uncle Jim and Amos got to the pond before Sam did, and Uncle Jim hollered out, 'Well, Sam, we beat you this time.' Uncle Jim never got tired tellin' what happened next. He said Sam run up the embankment with his spade, and set it in the ground and put his foot on it to push it down. The next minute he give a yell that you could 'a' heard half a mile, slung the spade over in the middle o' the pond, jumped three feet in the air, and run down the embankment yellin' and kickin' and throwin' his arms about in every direction, and at last he fell down on the ground a good distance from the pond.

"Amos and Uncle Jim was so taken by surprise at first that they jest stood still and looked. Amos says, says he: 'The man's gone crazy all at once.' Uncle Jim says: 'He's havin' a spell. His father and grand-father before him used to have them spells.'

"They run up to him and found him shakin' like a leaf, the cold sweat streamin' out of every pore, and gaspin' and sayin', 'Take it away! Take it away!' and all the time he was throwin' out his left foot in every direction. Finally Uncle Jim grabbed hold of his foot and there was a red and black necktie stickin' out o' the leg of his pants. He pulled it out and says he: 'Why, Sam, what's your Sunday necktie doin' up your pants leg?'

"They said Sam looked at it in a foolish sort o' way and then he fell back laughin' and cryin' at the same time, jest like a woman, and it was five minutes or more before they could stop him. Uncle Jim brought water and put on his head, and Amos fanned him with his hat, and at last they got him in such a fix that he could sit up and talk, and says he:

"'I took off my necktie last night and slung it down

on a chair where my everyday pants was layin'. When I put my foot in my pants this mornin' I must 'a' carried the necktie inside, and by the time I got to the pond it'd worked down, and I thought it was a black snake with red stripes.'

"He started to git up, but his ankle was sprained, and Uncle Jim says: 'No wonder, Sam; you jumped about six feet when you saw that snake crawlin' out o' your pants leg.'

"And Sam says: 'Six feet? I know I jumped six hundred feet, Uncle Jim.'

"Well, they got him to the house and told Milly about it, and she says: 'Well, Sam, I'm too sorry for you to laugh at you like Uncle Jim, but I must say this wouldn't 'a' happened if you'd folded up that necktie and put it away in the top drawer.'

"Sam was settin' on the side of the bed rubbin' his ankle, and he give a groan and says he: 'Things has come to a fine pass in Kentucky when a sober, God-fearin' man like me has to put his necktie in the top drawer to keep from seein' snakes.'

"I declare to goodness!" laughed Aunt Jane, as she laid down her trowel and pushed back her calico sunbonnet, "if I never heard anything funny again in this world, I could keep on laughin' till I died jest over things I ricollect. The trouble is there ain't always anybody around to laugh with me. Sam Amos ain't nothin' but a name to you, child, but to me he's jest as rcal as if he hadn't been dead thcse many years, and I can laugh over the things he used to do the same as if they happened yesterday."

Only a name! And I had read it on a lichen-covered stone in the old burying-ground; but as I walked home through the twilight I would hardly have been startled if Sam Amos, in the pride of life, had come riding past me on his bay mare, or if Uncle Jim Matthews' voice of cheerful discord had mingled with the spring song of the frogs sounding from every marsh and pond.

It was Aunt Jane's motto that wherever a· weed would grow a flower would grow; and carrying out this principle of planting, her garden was continually extending its boundaries; and denizens of the garden proper were to be found in every nook and corner of her domain. In the spring you looked for grass only; and lo! starting up at your feet, like the unexpected joys of life, came the golden daffodil, the paler narcissus, the purple iris, and the red and yellow tulip, flourishing as bravely as in the soil of its native Holland; and for a few sunny weeks the front yard would be a great flower garden. Then blossom and leaf would fade, and you might walk all summer over the velvet grass, never knowing how much beauty and fragrance lay hidden in the darkness of the earth. But when I go back to Aunt Jane's garden, I pass through the front yard and the back yard between rows of lilac, syringas, calycanthus, and honeysuckle; I open the rickety gate, and find myself in a genuine old-fashioned garden, the homely, inclusive spot that welcomed all growing things to its hospitable bounds, type of the days when there were no impassable barriers of gold and caste between man and his brother man. In the middle of the garden stood a "summer-house," or arbor, whose crumbling timbers were knit together by interlacing branches of honeysuckle and running roses. The summer-house had four entrances, opening on four paths that divided the ground into quarter-sections occupied by vegetables and small fruits, and around these, like costly embroidery on the hem of a homespun garment, ran a wide border of flowers that blossomed from early April to late November, shifting from one beauty to another as each flower had its little day.

THE GARDENS OF MEMORY

There are flower-lovers who love some flowers and other flower-lovers who love all flowers. Aunt Jane was of the latter class. The commonest plant, striving in its own humble way to be sweet and beautiful, was sure of a place here, and the haughtiest aristocrat who sought admission had to lay aside all pride of place or birth and acknowledge her kinship with common humanity. The Bourbon rose could not hold aside her skirts from contact with the cabbage-rose; the lavender could not disdain the companionship of sage and thyme. All must live together in the concord of a perfect democracy. Then if the great Gardener bestowed rain and sunshine when they were needed, midsummer days would show a glorious symphony of color around the gray farmhouse, and through the enchantment of bloom and fragrance flitted an old woman, whose dark eyes glowed with the joy of living, and the joy of remembering all life's other summers.

To Aunt Jane every flower in the garden was a human thing with a life story, and close to the summer-house grew one historic rose, heroine of an old romance, to which I listened one day as we sat in the arbor, where hundreds of honeysuckle blooms were trumpeting their fragrance on the air.

267

"Grandmother's rose, child, that's all the name it's got," she said, in answer to my question. "I reckon you think a fine-lookin' rose like that ought to have a fine-soundin' name. But I never saw anybody yet that knew enough about roses to tell what its right name is. Maybe when I'm dead and gone somebody'll tack a French name on to it, but as long as it grows in my gyarden it'll be jest grandmother's rose, and this is how it come by the name:

"My grandfather and grandmother was amongst the first settlers of Kentucky. They come from the Old Dominion over the Wilderness Road way back yonder, goodness knows when. Did you ever think, child, how curious it was for them men to leave their homes and risk their own lives and the lives of their little children and their wives jest to git to a new country? It appears to me they must 'a' been led jest like Columbus was when he crossed the big ocean in his little ships. I reckon if the women and children had had their way about it, the bears and wildcats and Indians would be here yet. But a man goes where he pleases, and a woman's got to foller, and that's the way it was with grandfather and grandmother. I've heard mother say that grandmother cried for a week when she found she had to go, and every now and then she'd sob out, 'I wouldn't mind it so much if I could take my gyarden.' When they began packin' up their things, grandmother took up this rose and put it in an iron kittle and laid plenty of good rich earth around the roots.   Grandfather said the load they had to carry was heavy enough without puttin' in any useless things.   But grandmother says, says she: 'If you leave this rose behind, you can leave me, too.'   So the kittle and the rose went.   Four weeks they was on their way, and every time they come to a creek or a river or a spring, grandmother'd water her rose, and when they got to their journey's end, before they'd ever chopped a tree or laid a stone or broke ground, she cut the sod with an axe, and then she took grandfather's huntin' knife and dug a hole and planted her rose.   Grandfather cut some limbs off a beech tree and drove 'em into the ground all around it to keep it from bein' tramped down, and when that was done, grandmother says: 'Now build the house so's this rose'll stand on the right-hand side o' the front walk.   Maybe I won't die of homesickness if I can set on my front doorstep and see one flower from my old Virginia gyarden.'

"Well, grandmother didn't die of homesickness, nor

the rose either. The transplantin' was good for both of 'em. She lived to be n'nety years old, and when she died the house wouldn't hold the children and grandchildren and great-grandchildren that come to the funeral. And here's her rose growin' and bloomin' yet, like there wasn't any such things in the world as old age and death. And every spring I gether a basketful o' these pink roses and lay 'em on her grave over yonder in the old buryin'-ground.

"Some folks has family china and family silver that they're mighty proud of. Martha Crawford used to have a big blue and white bowl that belonged to her great-grandmother, and she thought more o' that bowl than she did of everything else in the house. Milly Amos had a set o' spoons that'd been in her family for four generations and was too precious to use; and I've got my family rose, and it's jest as dear to me as china and silver are to other folks. I ricollect after father died and the estate had to be divided up, and sister Mary and brother Joe and the rest of 'em was layin' claim to the claw-footed mahogany table and the old secretary and mother's cherry sideboard and such things as that, and brother Joe turned around and says to me, says he:

THE GARDENS OF MEMORY

"'Is there anything you want, Jane? If there is, speak up and make it known.' And I says: 'The rest of you can take what you want of the furniture, and if there's anything left, that can be my part. If there ain't anything left, there'll be no quarrelin'; for there's jest one thing I want, and that's grandmother's rose.'

"They all laughed, and sister Mary says, 'Ain't that jest like Jane?' and brother Joe says, says he:

"'You shall have it, Jane, and further than that, I'll see to the transplantin'.'

"'That very evenin' he come over, and I showed him where I wanted the rose to stand. He dug 'way down into the clay — there's nothin' a rose likes better, child, than good red clay — and got a wheelbarrer load o' soil from the woods, and we put that in first and set the roots in it and packed 'em good and firm, first with woods' soil, then with clay, waterin' it all the time. When we got through, I says: 'Now, you pretty thing you, if you could come all the way from Virginia in a old iron kittle, you surely won't mind bein' moved from father's place to mine. Now you've got to live and bloom for me same as you did for mother.'

"You needn't laugh, child. That rose knew jest what I said, and did jest what I told it to do. It looked

271

like everything favored us, for it was early in the spring, things was beginnin' to put out leaves, and the next day was cloudy and cool. Then it began to rain, and rained for thirty-six hours right along. And when the sun come out, grandmother's rose come out, too. Not a leaf on it ever withered, and me and my children and my children's children have gethered flowers from it all these years. Folks say I'm foolish about it, and I reckon I am. I've outlived most o' the people I love, but I don't want to outlive this rose. We've both weathered many a hard winter, and two or three times it's been winter-killed clean to the ground, and I thought I'd lost it. Honey, it was like losin' a child. But there's never been a winter yet hard enough to kill the life in that rose's root, and I trust there never will be while I live, for spring wouldn't be spring to me without grandmother's rose."

Tall, straight, and strong it stood, this oft trans-planted pilgrim rose; and whether in bloom or clothed only in its rich green foliage, you saw at a glance that it was a flower of royal lineage. When spring covered it with buds and full blown blossoms of pink, the true rose color, it spoke of queens' gardens and kings' palaces, and every satiny petal was a palimpsest of song and legend. Its perfume was the attar-of-rose scent, like that of the roses of India. It satisfied and satiated with its rich potency. And breathing this odor and gazing into its deep wells of color, you had strange dreams of those other pilgrims who left home and friends, and journeyed through the perils of a trackless wilderness to plant still farther westward the rose of civilization.

To Aunt Jane there were three epochs in a garden's life, "daffodil time," "rose time," and "chrysanthemum time"; and the blossoming of all other flowers would be chronicled under one of these periods, just as we say of historical events that they happened in the reign of this or that queen or empress. But this garden had all seasons for its own, and even in winter there was a deep pleasure in walking its paths and noting how bravely life struggled against death in the frozen bosom of the earth.

I once asked her which flower she loved best. It was "daffodil time," and every gold cup held nepenthe for the nightmare dream of winter. She glanced reprovingly at me over her spectacles.

"It appears to me, child, you ought to know that without askin'," she said. "Did you ever see as many daffydils in one place before? No; and you never will. I've been plantin' that flower every spring for sixty years, and I've never got too many of 'em yet. I used to call 'em Johnny-jump-ups, till Henrietta told me that their right name was daffydil. But Johnny-jump-up suits 'em best, for it kind o' tells how they come up in the spring. The hyacinths and tulips, they hang back till they know it'll be warm and comfortable outside, but these daffydils don't wait for anything. Before the snow's gone you'll see their leaves pushin' up through the cold ground, and the buds come hurryin' along tryin' to keep up with the leaves, jest like they knew that little children and old women like me was waitin' and longin' for 'em. Why, I've seen these flowers bloomin' and the snow fallin' over 'em in March, and they didn't mind it a bit. I got my start o' daffydils from mother's gyarden, and every fall I'd divide the roots up and scatter 'em out till I got the whole place pretty well sprinkled with 'em, but the biggest part of 'em come from the old Harris farm, three or four miles down the pike. Forty years ago that farm was sold, and the man that bought it tore things up scandalous. He called it remodelin', I ricollect, but it looked more like ruinin' to me. Old Lady Harris was like myself;

she couldn't git enough of these yeller flowers. She had a double row of 'em all around her gyarden, and they'd even gone through the fence and come up in the cornfield, and who ever plowed that field had to be careful not to touch them daffydils.

"Well, as soon as the new man got possession he begun plowin' up the gyarden, and one evenin' the news come to me that he was throwin' away Johnny-jump-ups by the wagon-load. I put on my sunbonnet and went out where Abram was at work in the field, and says I, 'Abram, you've got to stop plowin' and put the horse to the spring wagon and take me over to the old Harris place.' And Abram says, says he, 'Why, Jane, I'd like mighty well to finish this field before night, for it looks like it might rain to-morrow. Is it anything particular you want to go for?'

"Says I, 'Yes; I never was so particular about anything in my life as I am about this. I hear they're plowin' up Old Lady Harris' gyarden and throwin' the flowers away, and I want to go over and git a wagon-load o' Johnny-jump-ups.'

"Abram looked at me a minute like he thought I was losin' my senses, and then he burst out laughin', and says he: 'Jane, who ever heard of a farmer stoppin' plowin' to go after Johnny-jump-ups? And who ever heard of a farmer's wife askin' him to do such a thing?'

"I walked up to the plow and begun to unfasten the trace chains, and says I: 'Business before pleasure, Abram. If it's goin' to rain to-morrow that's all the more reason why I ought to have my Johnny-jump-ups set out to-day. The plowin' can wait till we come back.'

"Of course Abram give in when he saw how I wanted the flowers. But he broke out laughin' two or three times while he was hitchin' up and says he: 'Don't tell any o' the neighbors, Jane, that I stopped plowin' to go after a load of Johnny-jump-ups.'

"When we got to the Harris place we found the Johnny-jump-ups lyin' in a gully by the side o' the road, a pitiful sight to anybody that loves flowers and understands their feelin's. We loaded up the wagon with the pore things, and as soon as we got home, Abram took his hoe and made a little trench all around the gyarden, and I set out the Johnny-jump-ups while Abram finished his plowin', and the next day the rain fell on Abram's cornfield and on my flowers.

"Do you see that row o' daffydils over yonder by the front fence, child — all leaves and no blossoms?' "

THE GARDENS OF MEMORY

I looked in the direction of her pointing finger and saw a long line of flowerless plants, standing like sad and silent guests at the festival of spring.

"It's been six years since I set 'em out there," said Aunt Jane impressively, "and not a flower have they had in all that time. Some folks say it's because I moved 'em at the wrong time o' the year. But the same week I moved these I moved some from my yard to Elizabeth Crawford's, and Elizabeth's bloom every year, so it can't be that. Some folks said the place I had 'em in was too shady, and I put 'em right out there where the sun strikes on 'em till it sets, and still they won't bloom. It's my opinion, honey, that they're jest homesick. I believe if I was to take them daffydils back to Aunt Matilda's and plant 'em in the border where they used to grow, alongside o' the sage and lavender and thyme, that they'd go to bloomin' again jest like they used to. You know how the children of Israel pined and mourned when they was carried into captivity. Well, every time I look at my daffydils I think o' them homesick Israelites askin', 'How can we sing the songs o' Zion in a strange land?'

"You needn't laugh, child. A flower is jest as human as you and me. Look at that vine yonder, takin' hold of everything that comes in its way like a little child learnin' to walk. And calycanthus buds, see how you've got to hold 'em in your hands and warm 'em before they'll give out their sweetness, jest like children that you've got to love and pet, before they'll let you git acquainted with 'em. You see that pink rose over by the fence?" pointing to a La France heavy with blossoms. "Well, that rose didn't do anything but put out leaves the first two years I had it. A bud might come once in a while, but it would blast before it was half open. And at last I says to it, says I, 'What is it you want, honey? There's somethin' that don't please you, I know. Don't you like the place you're planted in, and the hollyhocks and lilies for neighbors?' And one day I took it up and set it between that white tea and another La France, and it went to bloomin' right away. It didn't like the neighborhood it was in, you see. And did you ever hear o' people disappearin' from their homes and never bein' found any more? Well, flowers can disappear the same way. The year before I was married there was a big bed o' pink chrysanthemums growin' under the dinin'-room windows at old Dr. Pendleton's. It wasn't a common magenta pink, it was as clear, pretty a pink as that La France rose. Well, I

278

saw 'em that fall for the first time and the last. The next year there wasn't any, and when I asked where they'd gone to, nobody could tell anything about 'em. And ever since then I've been searchin' in every old gyarden in the county, but I've never found 'em, and I don't reckon I ever will.

"And there's my roses! Just look at 'em! Every color a rose could be, and pretty near every kind there is. Wouldn't you think I'd be satisfied? But there's a rose I lost sixty years ago, and the ricollection o' that rose keeps me from bein' satisfied with all I've got. It grew in Old Lady Elrod's gyarden and nowhere else, and there ain't a rose here except grandmother's that I wouldn't give up forever if I could jest find that rose again.

"I've tried many a time to tell folks about that rose, but I can't somehow get hold of the words. I reckon an old woman like me, with little or no learnin', couldn't be expected to tell how that rose looked, any more'n she could be expected to draw it and paint it. I can say it was yeller, but that word 'yeller' don't tell the color the rose was. I've got all the shades of yeller in my garden, but nothin' like the color o' that rose. It got deeper and deeper towards the middle, and lookin' at one of them roses half-opened was like lookin' down into a gold mine. The leaves crinkled and curled back towards the stem as fast as it opened, and the more it opened the prettier it was, like some women that grow better lookin' the older they grow, — Mary Andrews was one o' that kind, — and when it comes to tellin' you how it smelt, I'll jest have to stop. There never was anything like it for sweetness, and it was a different sweetness from any other rose God ever made.

"I ricollect seein' Miss Penelope come in church one Sunday, dressed in white, with a black velvet gyirdle 'round her waist, and a bunch o' these roses, buds and half-blown ones and full-blown ones, fastened in the gyirdle, and that bunch o' yeller roses was song and sermon and prayer to me that day. I couldn't take my eyes off 'em; and I thought that if Christ had seen that rose growin' in the fields around Palestine, he wouldn't 'a' mentioned lilies when he said Solomon in all his glory was not arrayed like one of these.

"I always intended to ask for a slip of it, but I waited too long. It got lost one winter, and when I asked Old Lady Elrod about it she said, 'Mistress Parrish, I cannot tell you whence it came nor whither it went.' The old lady always used mighty pretty language.

THE GARDENS OF MEMORY

"Well, honey, them two lost flowers jest haunt me. They're like dead children. You know a house may be full o' livin' children, but if there's one dead, a mother'll see its face and hear its voice above all the others, and that's the way with my lost flowers. No matter how many roses and chrysanthemums I have, I keep seein' Old Lady Elrod's yeller roses danglin' from Miss Penelope's gyirdle, and that bed o' pink chrysanthemums under Dr. Pendleton's dinin'-room windows."

"Each mortal has his Carcassonne!" Here was Aunt Jane's, but it was no matter for a tear or even a sigh. And I thought how the sting of life would lose its venom, if for every soul the unattainable were embodied in nothing more embittering than two exquisite lost flowers.

One afternoon in early June I stood with Aunt Jane in her garden. It was the time of roses; and in the midst of their opulent bloom stood the tall white lilies, handmaidens to the queen. Here and there over the warm earth old-fashioned pinks spread their prayer-rugs, on which a worshiper might kneel and offer thanks for life and spring; and towering over all, rows of many-colored hollyhocks flamed and glowed in the light of the setting sun like the stained glass windows of some old cathedral.

Across the flowery expanse Aunt Jane looked wistfully toward the evening skies, beyond whose stars and clouds we place that other world called heaven.

"I'm like my grandmother, child," she said presently. "I know I've got to leave this country some day soon, and journey to another one, and the only thing I mind about it is givin' up my gyarden. When John looked into heaven he saw gold streets and gates of pearl, but he don't say anything about gyardens. I like what he says about no sorrer, nor cryin', nor pain, and God wipin' away all tears from their eyes. That's pure comfort. But if I could jest have Abram and the children again, and my old home and my old gyarden, I'd be willin' to give up the gold streets and glass sea and pearl gates."

The loves of earth and the homes of earth! No apocalyptic vision can come between these and the earth-born human heart.

Life is said to have begun in a garden; and if here was our lost paradise, may not the paradise we hope to gain through death be, to the lover of nature, another garden in a new earth, girdled by four soft-flowing rivers, and watered by mists that arise in the night to fall on the face of the sleeping world, where all we plant shall grow unblighted through winterless years, and they who inherit it go with white garments and shining faces, and say at morn and noon and eve: *My soul is like a watered garden?*

CPSIA information can be obtained
at www.ICGtesting.com
Printed in the USA
BVHW042054170119
538096BV00010B/375/P